Toddler Girls and Boys Grade Guide

Size	2T–3T		3T–4T	
	Difference Between Sizes in Inches (Fractions/Decimals)			
Neck Circumference	3/8	.375	3/8	.375
Shoulder Length	1/8	.125	1/8	.125
Across Shoulder	1/2	.5	1/2	.5
Center Back Length (For Tops)	1	1	1	1
Front Torso Length (HPS to Crotch)	2 1/4	2.25	2 1/4	2.25
Across Back	1/2	.5	1/2	.5
Across Chest	1	1	1	1
Across Waist	1	1	1	1
Armhole Circumference	1/2	.5	1/2	.5
Upper Sleeve Width	1/2	.5	1/2	.5
Sleeve Length (For Short Sleeve)	3/4	.75	3/4	.75
Sleeve Length (For Long Sleeve)	1 1/4	1.25	1 1/4	1.25
Sleeve Hem/Cuff Opening	1/8	.125	1/8	.125
Hip Circumference	1	1	1	1
Total Rise	1 1/8	1.125	1 1/8	1.125
Thigh Circumference	5/8	.625	5/8	.625
Inseam	1/4	.25	1/4	.25
Ankle Circumference	3/8	.375	3/8	.375

Unless a front or back measurement is indicated, all grade rules reflect incremental differences between total measurements.

Infant Girls and Boys Grade Guide

Size	0–3 & 3–6 mos.		3–6 & 6–9 mos.		6–9 & 9–12 mos.		12 & 18 mos.	
	Difference Between Sizes in Inches (Fractions/Decimals)							
Neck Circumference	1/4	.25	1/4	.25	1/4	.25	1/2	.5
Shoulder Length	1/8	.125	1/8	.125	1/8	.125	1/8	.125
Across Shoulder	1/4	.25	1/2	.5	1/2	.5	3/8	.375
Center Back Length (For Tops)	1/2	.5	1/2	.5	1/2	.5	1/2	.5
Front Torso Length (HPS to Crotch)	1 1/4	1.25	1 1/4	1.25	1 1/4	1.25	2	2
Across Back	1/4	.25	1/2	.5	1/2	.5	3/8	.375
Across Chest	1	1	1	1	3/4	.75	1	1
Across Waist	1	1	1	1	3/4	.75	1	1
Armhole Circumference	1/2	.5	1/2	.5	1/2	.5	1/2	.5
Upper Sleeve Width	1/4	.25	1/2	.5	1/2	.5	1/2	.5
Sleeve Length (For Short Sleeve)	1/4	.25	1/4	.25	1/2	.5	1/2	.5
Sleeve Length (For Long Sleeve)	5/8	.625	5/8	.625	5/8	.625	1	1
Sleeve Hem/Cuff Opening	0	0	1/8	.125	1/8	.125	1/8	.125
Hip Circumference	1	1	1	1	3/4	.75	1	1
Total Rise	1/2	.5	3/4	.75	3/4	.75	1 1/4	1.25
Thigh Circumference	5/8	.625	5/8	.625	5/8	.625	3/4	.75
Inseam	0	0	0	0	1/4	.25	1/4	.25
Ankle Circumference	1/8	.125	1/4	.25	1/4	.25	1/4	.25

Unless a front or back measurement is indicated, all grade rules reflect incremental differences between total measurements.

Preteen Boys 6–18 Grade Guide

Size	8 & 10		10 & 12		12 & 14		14 & 16		16 & 18		18 & 20	
	Difference Between Sizes in Inches (Fractions/Decimals)											
Neck Circumference	1/2	.5	1/2	.5	5/8	.625	3/4	.75	3/4	.75	3/4	.75
Shoulder Length	1/4	.25	1/4	.25	1/4	.25	1/4	.25	1/4	.25	1/4	.25
Across Shoulder	5/8	.625	5/8	.625	5/8	.625	1/2	.5	1/2	.5	1/2	.5
Center Back Length (For Tops)	1/2	.5	1/2	.5	3/4	.75	3/4	.75	3/4	.75	3/4	.75
Front Torso Length (HPS to Crotch)	3	3	3	3	3	3	3	3	2 1/2	2.5	2	2
Across Back	5/8	.625	5/8	.625	5/8	.625	1/2	.5	1/2	.5	1/2	.5
Across Chest	1 1/2	1.5	1 1/2	1.5	1 3/4	1.75	1 3/4	1.75	1 1/2	1.5	1 1/2	1.5
Across Waist	1	1	1	1	1	1	1	1	1	1	1	1
Armhole Circumference	3/4	.75	1	1	1	1	1	1	3/4	.75	3/4	.75
Upper Sleeve Width	1/2	.5	3/4	.75	3/4	.75	3/4	.75	1/2	.5	1/2	.5
Sleeve Length (For Short Sleeve)	1/2	.5	1/2	.5	1/2	.5	1/2	.5	1/2	.5	1/2	.5
Sleeve Length (For Long Sleeve)	1	1	1	1	1	1	1	1	1	1	1	1
Sleeve Hem/Cuff Opening	1/4	.25	1/4	.25	1/4	.25	1/4	.25	1/4	.25	1/4	.25
Hip Circumference	1 1/2	1.5	1 1/2	1.5	2	2	2	2	1 1/2	1.5	1 1/2	1.5
Total Rise	1 1/4	1.25	1 1/4	1.25	1 1/4	1.25	1 1/4	1.25	1	1	1	1
Thigh Circumference	1 1/4	1.25	1 1/4	1.25	1 1/4	1.25	1 1/4	1.25	1	1	1	1
Inseam	1 3/8	1.375	2	2	3/4	.75	3/4	.75	3/4	.75	3/4	.75
Ankle Circumference	1/2	.5	1/2	.5	1/2	.5	1/2	.5	3/8	.375	3/8	.375

Unless a front or back measurement is indicated, all grade rules reflect incremental differences between total measurements.

Children 4–6x Grade Guide

Size	4 & 5		5 & 6		6 & 6x	
	Difference Between Sizes in Inches (Fractions/Decimals)					
Neck Circumference	3/8	.375	3/8	.375	3/8	.375
Shoulder Length	1/8	.125	1/8	.125	1/8	.125
Across Shoulder	1/2	.5	1/2	.5	3/8	.375
Center Back Length (For Tops)	1	1	1	1	1	1
Front Torso Length (HPS to Crotch)	1 1/2	1.5	1 1/2	1.5	1 1/4	1.25
Across Back	1/2	.5	1/2	.5	3/8	.375
Across Chest	1	1	1	1	1	1
Across Waist	1/2	.5	1/2	.5	1/2	.5
Armhole Circumference	3/4	.75	3/4	.75	3/8	.375
Upper Sleeve Width	1/2	.5	1/2	.5	1/2	.5
Sleeve Length (For Short Sleeve)	1/2	.5	1/2	.5	1/2	.5
Sleeve Length (For Long Sleeve)	1	1	1	1	1	1
Sleeve Hem/Cuff Opening	1/8	.125	1/8	.125	1/8	.125
Hip Circumference	1	1	1	1	1	1
Total Rise	3/4	.75	3/4	.75	3/4	.75
Thigh Circumference	3/4	.75	3/4	.75	1/2	.5
Inseam	2	2	2	2	2	2
Ankle Circumference	3/8	.375	3/8	.375	3/8	.375

Unless a front or back measurement is indicated, all grade rules reflect incremental differences between total measurements.

Junior Grade Guide

Size	3 & 5		5 & 7		7 & 9		9 & 11		11 & 13	
	Difference Between Sizes in Inches (Fractions/Decimals)									
Neck Circumference	1/4	.25	1/4	.25	1/4	.25	3/8	.375	3/8	.375
Shoulder Length	3/8	.375	3/8	.375	1/8	.125	1/8	.125	1/8	.125
Across Shoulder	1/4	.25	1/4	.25	1/4	.25	1/4	.25	1/4	.25
Center Back Length (For Tops)	1/4	.25	1/4	.25	1/4	.25	1/4	.25	1/2	.5
Front Torso Length (HPS to Crotch)	1/4	.25	1/4	.25	1/4	.25	1 1/2	1.5	1 1/2	1.5
Across Back	1/8	.125	1/8	.125	1/4	.25	3/8	.375	3/8	.375
Across Chest	1	1	1	1	1	1	1 1/2	1.5	1 1/2	1.5
Across Waist	1	1	1	1	1	1	1 1/2	1.5	1 1/2	1.5
Armhole Circumference	3/8	.375	3/8	.375	3/8	.375	1/2	.5	1/2	.5
Upper Sleeve Width	1/8	.125	1/8	.125	3/8	.375	1/2	.5	1/2	.5
Sleeve Length (For Short Sleeve)	1/4	.25	1/4	.25	1/4	.25	1/4	.25	1/4	.25
Sleeve Length (For Long Sleeve)	3/8	.375	3/8	.375	3/8	.375	3/8	.375	3/8	.375
Sleeve Hem/Cuff Opening	1/2	.5	3/4	.75	1/8	.125	1/4	.25	1/4	.25
High Hip Circumference	1	1	1	1	1	1	1 1/2	1.5	1 1/2	1.5
Low Hip Circumference	1	1	1	1	1	1	1 1/2	1.5	1 1/2	1.5
Total Rise	3/4	.75	3/4	.75	3/4	.75	3/4	.75	3/4	.75
Thigh Circumference	1/4	.25	1/4	.25	1/4	.25	1	1	1	1
Inseam	1/4	.25	1/4	.25	1/4	.25	1/4	.25	1/4	.25
Ankle Circumference	1 1/2	1.5	1 1/2	1.5	1 1/2	1.5	1/4	.25	1/4	.25

Unless a front or back measurement is indicated, all grade rules reflect incremental differences between total measurements.

Preteen Girls 7–14 Grade Guide

Size	7 & 8		8 & 10		10 & 12		12 & 14	
	Difference Between Sizes in Inches (Fractions/Decimals)							
Neck Circumference	1/4	.25	1/2	.5	1/2	.5	1/2	.5
Shoulder Length	1/8	.125	1/8	.125	1/8	.125	1/8	.125
Across Shoulder	1/4	.25	1/2	.5	1/2	.5	1/2	.5
Center Back Length (For Tops)	1/2	.5	1/2	.5	3/4	.75	3/4	.75
Front Torso Length (HPS to Crotch)	2	2	2	2	2 1/2	2.5	2 1/2	2.5
Across Back	1/4	.25	1/2	.5	1/2	.5	1/2	.5
Across Chest	1	1	1 1/2	1.5	1 1/2	1.5	1 1/2	1.5
Across Waist	1/2	.5	1	1	1	1	1	1
Armhole Circumference	1/2	.5	1/2	.5	3/4	.75	3/4	.75
Upper Sleeve Width	3/8	.375	3/8	.375	3/8	.375	1/2	.5
Sleeve Length (For Short Sleeve)	3/8	.375	1/2	.5	1/2	.5	1/2	.5
Sleeve Length (For Long Sleeve)	3/4	.75	1	1	1	1	1	1
Sleeve Hem/Cuff Opening	1/4	.25	1/8	.125	1/8	.125	1/4	.25
Hip Circumference	1	1	1 1/2	1.5	2	2	2	2
Total Rise	3/4	.75	1 1/4	1.25	1 1/4	1.25	1 1/4	1.25
Thigh Circumference	1/2	.5	1	1	1 1/4	1.25	1 1/4	1.25
Inseam	1 3/8	1.375	1 3/8	1.375	2	2	3/4	.75
Ankle Circumference	3/8	.375	3/8	.375	3/8	.375	3/8	.375

Unless a front or back measurement is indicated, all grade rules reflect incremental differences between total measurements.

Petite Grade Guide

Size	4P & 6P		6P & 8P		8P & 10P		10P & 12P		12P & 14P	
	Difference Between Sizes in Inches (Fractions/Decimals)									
Neck Circumference	1/4	.25	1/4	.25	1/4	.25	3/8	.375	3/8	.375
Shoulder Length	1/8	.125	1/8	.125	1/8	.125	1/8	.125	1/8	.125
Across Shoulder	1/4	.25	1/4	.25	1/4	.25	3/8	.375	3/8	.375
Center Back Length (For Tops)	1/4	.25	1/4	.25	1/4	.25	1/4	.25	1/4	.25
Front Torso Length (HPS to Crotch)	1 1/2	1.5	1 1/2	1.5	1 1/2	1.5	1 1/2	1.5	1 1/2	1.5
Across Back	1/4	.25	1/4	.25	1/4	.25	3/8	.375	3/8	.375
Across Chest	1	1	1	1	1	1	1 1/2	1.5	1 1/2	1.5
Across Waist	1	1	1	1	1	1	1 1/2	1.5	1 1/2	1.5
Armhole Circumference	1/2	.5	1/2	.5	1/2	.5	3/4	.75	3/4	.75
Upper Sleeve Width	3/8	.375	3/8	.375	3/8	.375	1/2	.5	1/2	.5
Sleeve Length (For Short Sleeve)	1/4	.25	1/4	.25	1/4	.25	1/4	.25	1/4	.25
Sleeve Length (For Long Sleeve)	3/8	.375	3/8	.375	3/8	.375	3/8	.375	3/8	.375
Sleeve Hem/Cuff Opening	1/8	.125	1/8	.125	1/8	.125	1/8	.125	1/8	.125
High Hip Circumference	1	1	1	1	1	1	1 1/2	1.5	1 1/2	1.5
Low Hip Circumference	1	1	1	1	1	1	1 1/2	1.5	1 1/2	1.5
Total Rise	3/4	.75	3/4	.75	3/4	.75	3/4	.75	3/4	.75
Thigh Circumference	3/4	.75	3/4	.75	3/4	.75	1	1	1	1
Inseam	0	0	0	0	0	0	0	0	0	0
Ankle Circumference	1/4	.25	1/4	.25	1/4	.25	1/4	.25	1/4	.25

Unless a front or back measurement is indicated, all grade rules reflect incremental differences between total measurements.

Men's Grade Guide

Size	34R & 36R		36R & 38R		38R & 40R		40R & 42R		42R & 44R		44R & 46R	
	Difference Between Sizes in Inches (Fractions/Decimals)											
Neck Circumference	1/2	.5	1/2	.25	1/2	.5	1/2	.5	1/2	.5	1/2	.5
Shoulder Length	1/8	.125	1/8	.125	1/8	.125	1/8	.125	1/8	.125	1/8	.125
Across Shoulder	1/2	.5	1/2	.5	1/2	.5	1/2	.5	1/2	.5	1/2	.5
Center Back Length (For Tops)	1/4	.25	1/4	.25	1/2	.5	1/2	.5	1/2	.5	1/2	.5
Front Torso Length (HPS to Crotch)	1 1/2	1.5	1 1/2	1.5	1 1/2	1.5	1 1/2	1.5	1 1/2	1.5	1 1/2	1.5
Across Back	1/2	.5	1/2	.5	1/2	.5	1/2	.5	1/2	.5	1/2	.5
Across Chest	2	2	2	2	2	2	2	2	2	2	2	2
Across Waist	2	2	2	2	2	2	2	2	2	2	2	2
Armhole Circumference	3/4	.75	3/4	.75	1	1	1	1	1	1	1	1
Upper Sleeve Width	1/2	.5	1/2	.5	1/2	.5	1/2	.5	1/2	.5	1/2	.5
Sleeve Length (For Short Sleeve)	1/4	.25	1/4	.25	1/4	.25	1/4	.25	1/4	.25	1/4	.25
Sleeve Length (For Long Sleeve)	1/4	.25	1/4	.25	1/4	.25	1/4	.25	1/4	.25	1/4	.25
Sleeve Hem/Cuff Opening	1/4	.25	1/4	.25	1/4	.25	1/4	.25	1/4	.25	1/4	.25
Hip Circumference	2	2	2	2	2	2	2	2	2	2	2	2
Total Rise	3/4	.75	3/4	.75	3/4	.75	3/4	.75	3/4	.75	3/4	.75
Thigh Circumference	1/2	.5	1/2	.5	1/2	.25	1	1	1	1	1	1
Inseam	vary		vary		vary		vary		vary		vary	
Ankle Circumference	1/4	.25	1/4	.25	1/4	.25	1/4	.25	3/8	.375	3/8	.375

Unless a front or back measurement is indicated, all grade rules reflect incremental differences between total measurements.

Appendix G

Incremental Grade Guides

Missy Grade Guide

Size	4 & 6		6 & 8		8 & 10		10 & 12		12 & 14	
	Difference Between Sizes in Inches (Fractions/Decimals)									
Neck Circumference	3/8	.375	3/8	.375	3/8	.375	5/8	.625	5/8	.625
Shoulder Length	1/8	.125	1/8	.125	1/8	.125	1/8	.125	1/8	.125
Across Shoulder	1/4	.25	1/4	.25	1/4	.25	3/8	.375	3/8	.375
Center Back Length (For Tops)	1/4	.25	1/4	.25	1/4	.25	1/4	.25	1/4	.25
Front Torso Length (HPS to Crotch)	1 1/2	1.5	1 1/2	1.5	1 1/2	1.5	1 1/2	1.5	1 1/2	1.5
Across Back	1/4	.25	1/4	.25	1/4	.25	3/8	.375	3/8	.375
Across Chest	1	1	1	1	1	1	1 1/2	1.5	1 1/2	1.5
Across Waist	1	1	1	1	1	1	1 1/2	1.5	1 1/2	1.5
Armhole Circumference	1/2	.5	1/2	.5	1/2	.5	3/4	.75	3/4	.75
Upper Sleeve Width	1/4	.25	1/4	.25	1/4	.25	3/8	.375	3/8	.375
Sleeve Length (For Short Sleeve)	1/4	.25	1/4	.25	1/4	.25	1/4	.25	1/4	.25
Sleeve Length (For Long Sleeve)	3/8	.375	3/8	.375	3/8	.375	3/8	.375	3/8	.375
Sleeve Hem/Cuff Opening	1/8	.125	1/8	.125	1/8	.125	1/4	.25	1/4	.25
High Hip Circumference	1	1	1	1	1	1	1 1/2	1.5	1 1/2	1.5
Low Hip Circumference	1	1	1	1	1	1	1 1/2	1.5	1 1/2	1.5
Total Rise	3/4	.75	3/4	.75	3/4	.75	3/4	.75	3/4	.75
Thigh Circumference	3/4	.75	3/4	.75	1	1	1	1	1	1
Inseam	1/4	.25	1/4	.25	1/4	.25	1/4	.25	1/4	.25
Ankle Circumference	1/4	.25	1/4	.25	1/4	.25	1/4	.25	1/4	.25

Unless a front or back measurement is indicated, all grade rules reflect incremental differences between total measurements.

Plus Size Grade Guide

Size	16W & 18W		18W & 20W		20W & 22W		24W & 24W		24W & 26W	
	Difference Between Sizes in Inches (Fractions/Decimals)									
Neck Circumference	1/2	.5	1/2	.5	1/2	.5	1/2	.5	1/2	.5
Shoulder Length	1/8	.125	1/8	.125	1/8	.125	1/8	.125	1/8	.125
Across Shoulder	1/2	.5	1/2	.5	1/2	.5	1/2	.5	3/8	.375
Center Back Length (For Tops)	1/4	.25	1/4	.25	1/4	.25	1/4	.25	1/4	.25
Front Torso Length (HPS to Crotch)	1 1/2	1.5	1 1/2	1.5	1 1/2	1.5	1 1/4	1.25	1 1/4	1.25
Across Back	1/2	.5	1/2	.5	1/2	.5	1/2	.5	1/2	.5
Across Chest	2	2	2	2	2	2	2	2	2	2
Across Waist	2	2	2	2	2	2	2	2	2	2
Armhole Circumference	3/4	.75	3/4	.75	3/4	.75	3/4	.75	3/4	.75
Upper Sleeve Width	5/8	.625	5/8	.625	5/8	.625	5/8	.625	5/8	.625
Sleeve Length (For Short Sleeve)	1/8	.125	1/8	.125	1/8	.125	1/8	.125	1/8	.125
Sleeve Length (For Long Sleeve)	1/4	.25	1/4	.25	1/4	.25	1/4	.25	1/4	.25
Sleeve Hem/Cuff Opening	1/4	.25	1/4	.25	1/4	.25	1/4	.25	1/4	.25
High Hip Circumference	2	2	2	2	2	2	2	2	2	2
Low Hip Circumference	2	2	2	2	2	2	2	2	2	2
Total Rise	3/4	.75	3/4	.75	3/4	.75	3/4	.75	3/4	.75
Thigh Circumference	1 1/4	1.25	1 1/4	1.25	1 1/4	1.25	1 1/4	1.25	1 1/4	1.25
Inseam	0	0	0	0	0	0	0	0	0	0
Ankle Circumference	1/4	.25	1/4	.25	1/4	.25	1/4	.25	1/4	.25

Unless a front or back measurement is indicated, all grade rules reflect incremental differences between total measurements.

Grading Worksheet

Style #: _____

NAME:		DATE:	SEASON:
DESCRIPTION:			
SAMPLE SIZE:			

SIZE RANGE

	Tol(+)	Tol(−)							

COLOR

SIZE ASSORTMENT

Appendix E

Fraction-to-Decimal Conversion Chart

Decimal	X/16th	X/8th	X/4th	X2th
.0625	1/16			
.125	2/16	1/8		
.1875	3/16			
.25	4/16	2/8	1/4	
.3125	5/16			
.375	6/16	3/8		
.4375	7/16			
.5	8/16	4/8	2/4	1/2
.5625	9/16			
.625	10/16	5/8		
.6875	11/16			
.75	12/16	6/8	3/4	
.8125	13/16			
.875	14/16	7/8		
.9375	15/16			
1.00	16/16	8/8	4/4	2/2

Metric Conversion Table (Inches to Centimeters)

Inches		1/16	1/8	1/4	3/8	1/2	5/8	3/4	7/8
		0.16	0.32	0.64	0.95	1.27	1.59	1.91	2.22
1	2.54	2.70	2.86	3.18	3.49	3.81	4.13	4.45	4.76
2	5.08	5.24	5.40	5.72	6.03	6.35	6.67	6.99	7.30
3	7.62	7.78	7.04	8.26	8.57	8.89	9.21	9.53	9.84
4	10.16	10.32	10.48	10.80	11.11	11.43	11.75	12.07	12.38
5	12.70	12.86	13.02	13.34	13.65	13.97	14.29	14.61	14.92
6	15.24	15.40	15.56	15.88	16.19	16.51	16.83	17.15	17.46
7	17.78	17.94	18.10	18.42	18.73	19.05	19.37	19.69	20.00
8	20.32	20.48	20.64	20.96	21.27	21.59	21.91	22.23	22.54
9	22.86	23.02	23.18	23.50	23.81	24.13	24.45	24.77	25.08
10	25.40	25.56	25.72	26.04	26.35	26.67	26.99	27.31	27.62
11	27.94	28.10	28.26	28.58	28.89	29.21	29.53	29.85	30.16
12	30.48	30.64	30.80	31.12	31.43	31.75	32.02	32.39	32.70
13	33.02	33.18	33.34	33.66	33.97	34.29	34.61	34.93	35.24
14	35.56	35.72	35.88	36.20	36.51	36.83	37.15	37.47	37.78
15	38.10	38.26	38.42	38.74	39.05	39.37	36.69	40.01	40.32
16	40.64	40.80	40.96	41.28	41.59	41.91	42.23	42.55	42.86
17	43.18	43.34	43.50	43.82	44.13	44.45	44.77	45.09	45.40
18	45.72	45.88	46.04	46.36	46.67	46.99	47.31	47.63	47.94
19	48.26	48.42	48.58	48.90	49.21	49.53	49.85	50.17	50.48
20	50.80	50.96	51.12	51.44	51.75	52.07	52.39	52.71	53.02
21	53.34	53.50	53.66	53.98	54.29	54.61	54.93	55.25	55.56
22	55.88	56.04	56.20	56.52	56.83	57.15	57.47	57.79	58.10
23	58.42	58.58	58.74	59.06	59.37	59.69	60.01	60.33	60.64
24	60.96	61.12	61.28	61.60	61.91	62.23	62.55	62.87	63.18
25	63.50	63.66	63.82	64.14	64.45	64.77	65.09	65.41	65.72
26	66.04	66.20	66.36	66.68	66.99	67.31	67.63	67.95	68.26
27	68.58	68.74	68.90	69.22	69.53	69.85	70.17	70.49	70.80
28	71.12	71.28	71.44	71.76	72.07	72.39	72.71	73.03	73.34
29	73.66	73.82	73.98	74.30	74.61	74.93	75.25	75.57	75.88
30	76.20	76.36	76.52	76.84	77.15	77.47	77.79	78.11	78.42
31	78.74	78.90	79.06	79.38	79.69	80.01	80.33	80.65	80.96
32	81.28	81.44	81.60	81.92	82.23	82.55	82.87	83.19	83.50
33	83.82	83.98	84.14	84.46	84.77	85.09	85.41	85.73	86.04
34	86.36	86.52	86.68	87.00	87.31	87.63	87.95	88.27	88.58
35	88.90	89.06	89.22	89.54	89.85	90.17	90.49	90.81	91.12
36	91.44	91.60	91.76	92.08	92.39	92.71	93.03	93.35	93.66
37	93.98	94.14	94.30	94.62	94.93	95.25	95.57	95.89	96.20
38	96.52	96.68	96.84	97.16	97.47	97.79	98.11	98.43	98.74
39	99.06	99.22	99.38	99.70	100.01	100.33	100.65	100.97	101.28
40	101.60	101.76	101.92	102.24	102.55	102.87	103.19	103.51	103.82
41	104.14	104.30	104.46	104.78	105.09	105.41	105.73	106.05	106.36
42	106.68	106.84	107.00	107.32	107.63	107.95	108.27	108.59	108.90
43	109.22	109.38	109.54	109.86	110.17	110.49	110.81	111.13	111.44
44	111.76	111.92	112.08	112.40	112.71	113.03	113.35	113.67	113.98
45	114.30	114.46	114.62	114.94	115.25	115.57	115.89	116.21	116.52
46	116.84	117.00	117.16	117.48	117.79	118.11	118.43	118.75	119.06
47	119.38	119.54	119.70	120.02	120.33	120.65	120.97	121.29	121.60
48	121.92	122.08	122.24	122.56	122.87	123.19	123.51	123.83	124.14
49	124.46	124.62	124.78	125.10	125.41	125.73	126.05	126.37	126.68
50	127.00	127.16	127.32	127.64	127.95	128.27	128.59	128.91	129.22
51	129.54	129.70	129.86	130.18	130.49	130.81	131.13	131.45	131.76
52	132.08	132.24	132.40	132.72	133.03	133.35	133.67	133.99	134.30
53	134.62	134.78	134.94	135.26	135.57	135.89	136.21	136.53	136.84
54	137.16	137.32	137.48	137.80	138.11	138.43	138.75	139.07	139.38
55	139.70	139.86	140.02	140.34	140.65	140.97	141.29	141.61	141.92
56	142.24	142.40	142.56	142.88	143.19	143.51	143.83	144.15	144.46
57	144.78	144.94	145.10	145.42	145.73	146.05	146.37	146.69	147.00
58	147.32	147.48	147.64	147.96	148.27	148.59	148.91	149.23	149.54
59	149.86	150.02	150.18	150.50	150.81	151.13	151.45	151.77	152.08
60	152.40	152.56	152.72	153.04	153.35	153.67	153.99	154.31	154.62

Graph Template—Centimeters

Appendix A

Button Selector Gauge

Buttons are measured in lignes

Button Sizes in Lignes

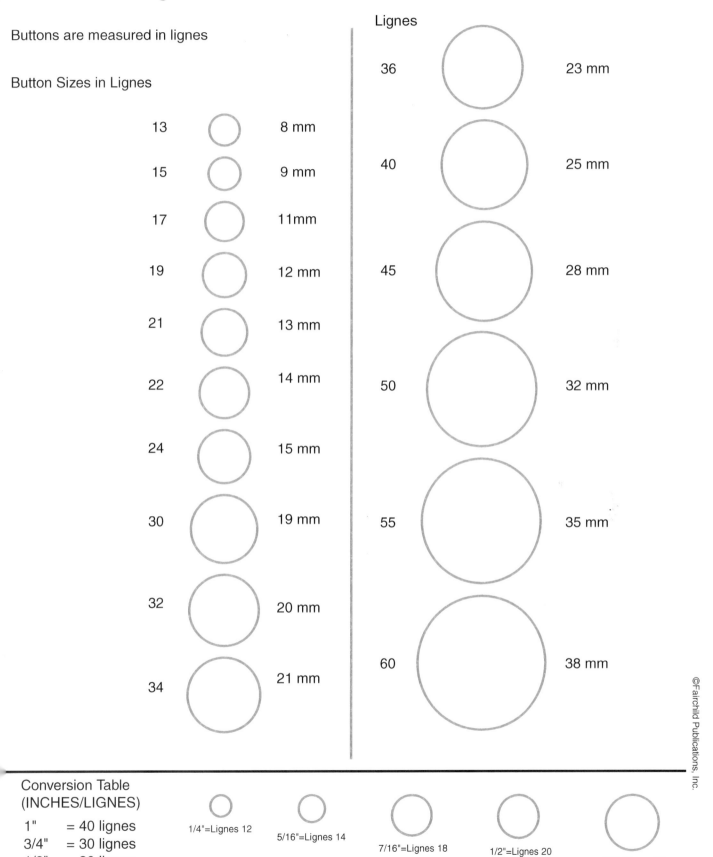

Lignes

Lignes		mm
13		8 mm
15		9 mm
17		11mm
19		12 mm
21		13 mm
22		14 mm
24		15 mm
30		19 mm
32		20 mm
34		21 mm

Lignes		mm
36		23 mm
40		25 mm
45		28 mm
50		32 mm
55		35 mm
60		38 mm

Conversion Table
(INCHES/LIGNES)

1"   = 40 lignes
3/4" = 30 lignes
1/2" = 20 lignes

1/4"=Lignes 12

5/16"=Lignes 14

7/16"=Lignes 18

1/2"=Lignes 20

5/8"=Lignes 24

Brush/Stitch Library

Zipper #1

Zipper #2

Zipper Teeth #1

Chain Stitch

Eyelet Beading

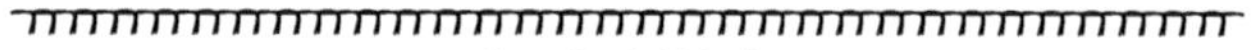

Overlock Stitch

Serge Stitch #1

Serge Stitch #2

Flat Lock Stitch

Overlock Stitch

Single Needle Top Stitch

Double Needle Top Stitch

Multi-Needle Top Stitch

Scallop

Scallop Edge

1 x 1 Rib

2 x 2 Rib

3 x 3 Rib

1 x 2 Rib

Cable

Casing #1

Casing #2

Casing #3

Gathers

**Single
Welt**

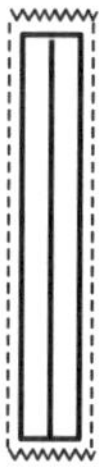

**Double Welt
(Besom)**

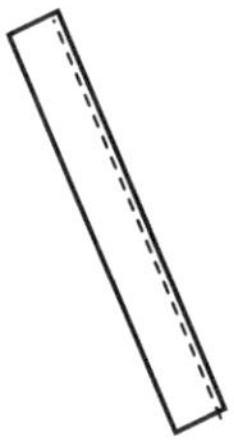

**Angled
Welt**

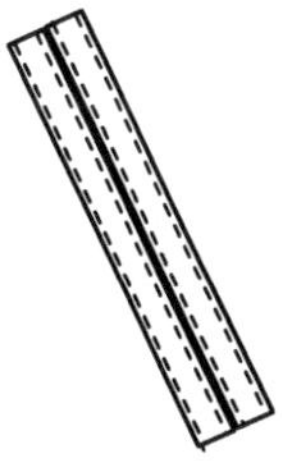

**Angled
Double Welt**

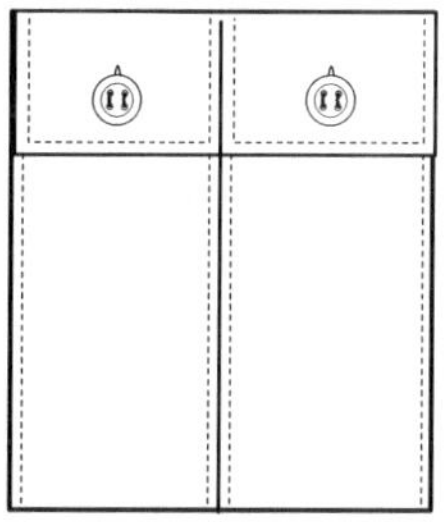

**Double Patch
with Button
Through Flap**

Patch with Flap

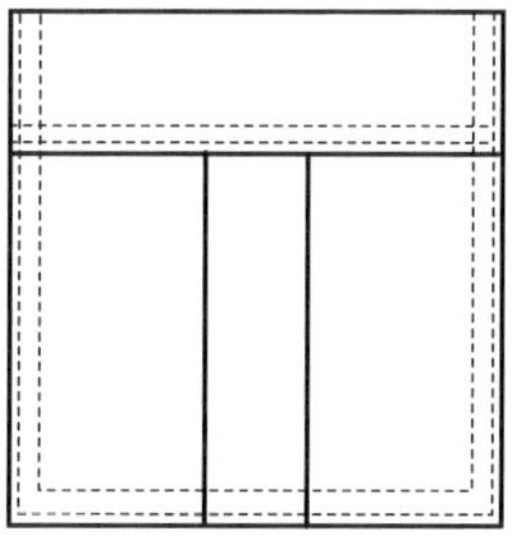

**Patch
with Pleat**

**Button through
Welt**

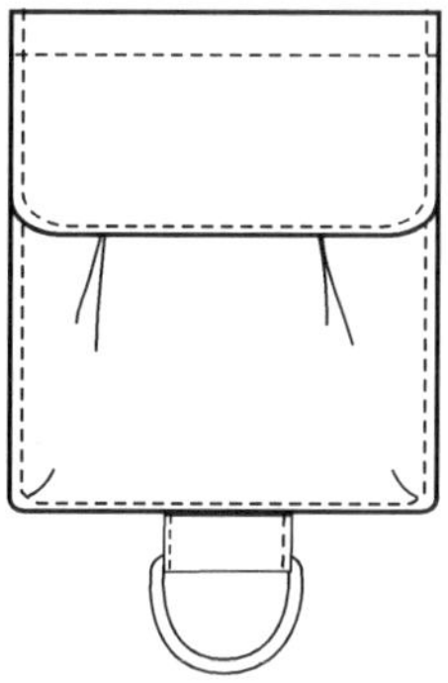

**Fatigue
with D-Ring**

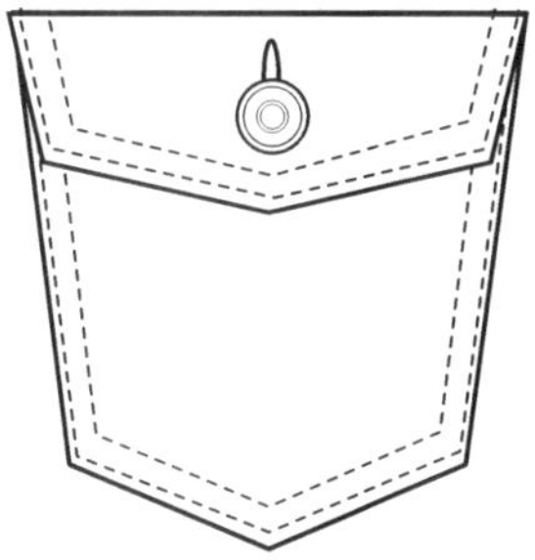

**Patch with Flap
and Point**

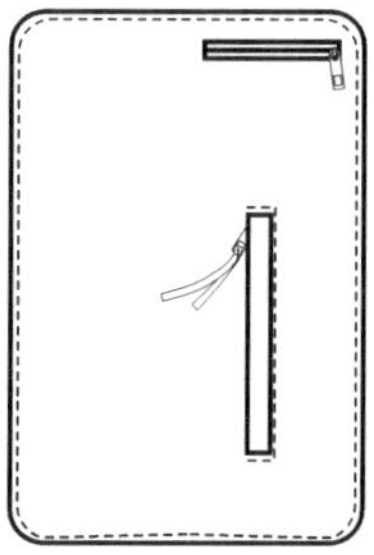

**Squircle
with Welt**

Smile

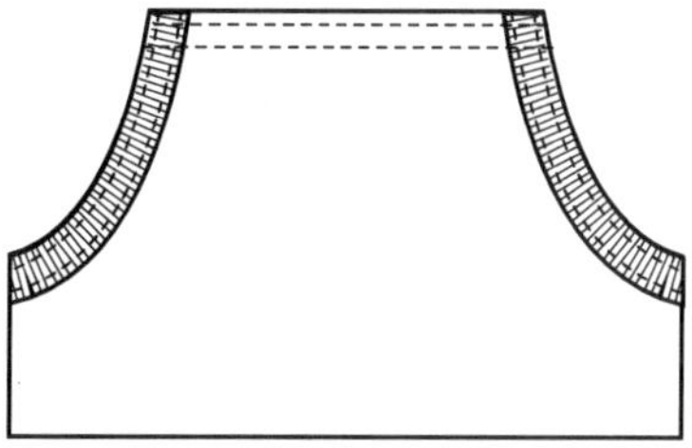

Kangaroo

Collars

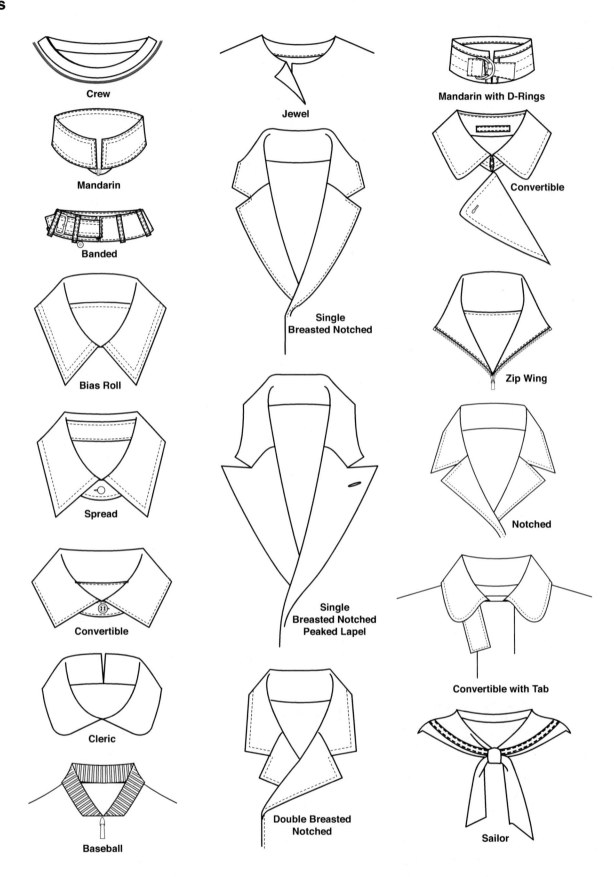

Crew

Mandarin

Banded

Bias Roll

Spread

Convertible

Cleric

Baseball

Jewel

Single
Breasted Notched

Single
Breasted Notched
Peaked Lapel

Double Breasted
Notched

Mandarin with D-Rings

Convertible

Zip Wing

Notched

Convertible with Tab

Sailor

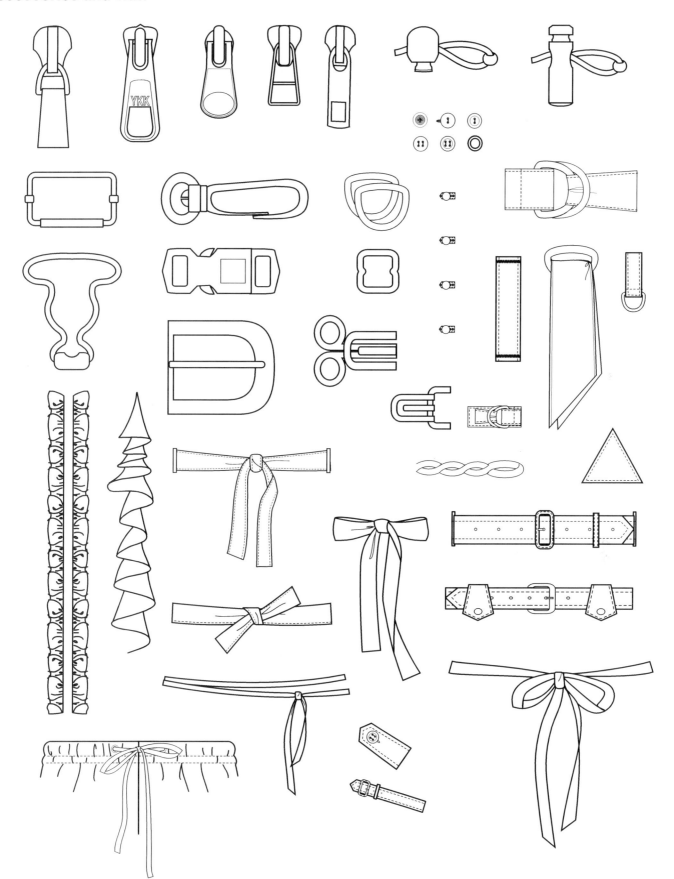

1 Year Old Flats

Dress

Snap Front Cardigan

Bunting

Outerwear

Polo Onesie

Woven Shirt

Underwear

Sweater

Skirt

Bodysuit

Tee Shirt

Shorts

All flats are drawn on croquis figures at 75% scale.

Tailored Jacket

Outerwear

Overalls

Tee Shirt

Bathing Suit

Skirt

Woven Shirt

Sweat Shirt

Dress

Pants

©Fairchild Publications, Inc.

All flats are drawn on croquis figures at 75% scale.

4–6x Flats

Outerwear

Sweater

Vest

Tailored Jacket

Woven Shirt

Bodysuit

Dress

Pants

Skirt

All flats are drawn on croquis figures at 75% scale.

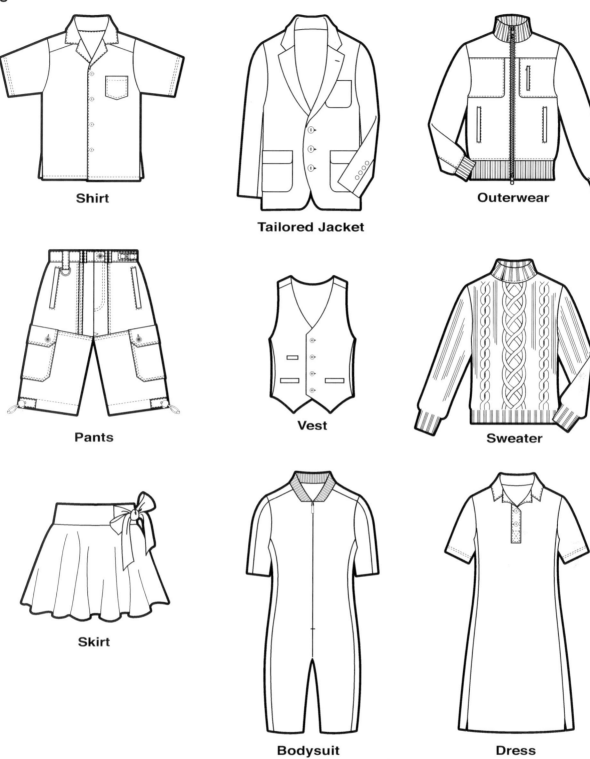

Shirt

Tailored Jacket

Outerwear

Pants

Vest

Sweater

Skirt

Bodysuit

Dress

All flats are drawn on croquis figures at 75% scale.

Preteen Flats

Tailored Jacket

Shirt

Vest

Pants

Bodysuit

Skirt

Dress

Outerwear

Sweater

All flats are drawn on croquis figures at 75% scale.

Jumpsuit

Sweater

Outerwear

Tailored Jacket

Shirt

Pants

Vest

Dress

Skirt

All flats are drawn on croquis figures at 75% scale.

Outerwear

Tailored Jacket

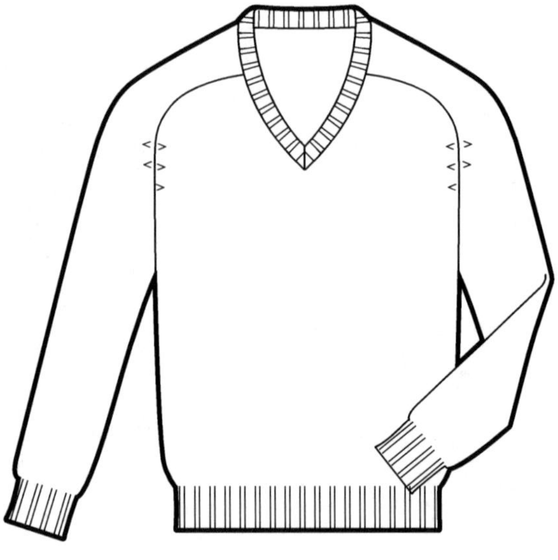

Sweater

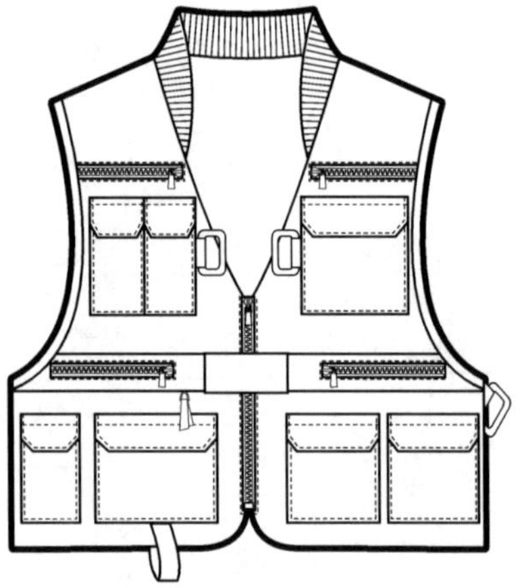

Vest

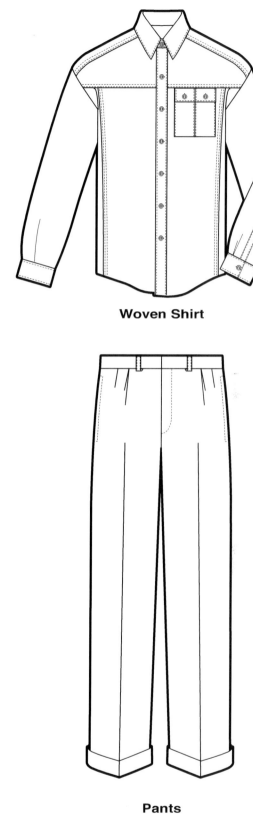

Unionsuit

Woven Shirt

Pants

All flats are drawn on croquis figures at 75% scale.

Dress

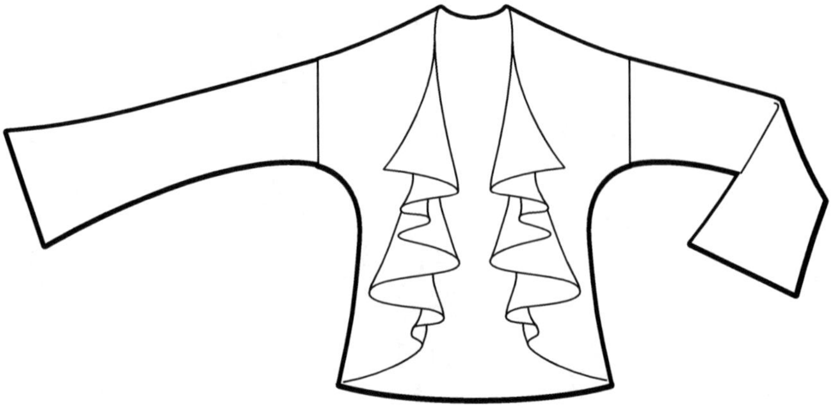

Tailored Jacket

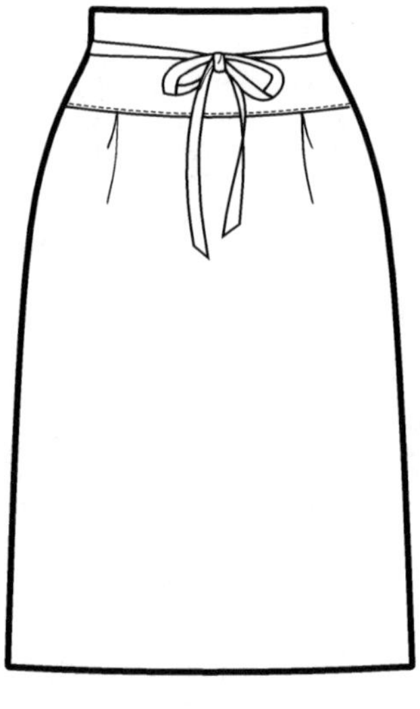

Skirt

Bodysuit

Woven Shirt

Vest

Outerwear

Pants

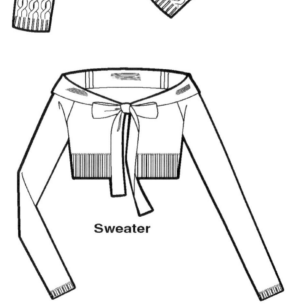

Sweater

All flats are drawn on croquis figures at 75% scale.

Plus Size Flats II

Bodysuit

Woven Shirt

Sweater

Vest

Pants

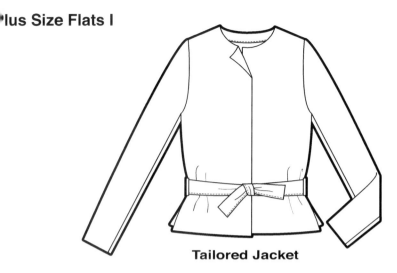

Tailored Jacket

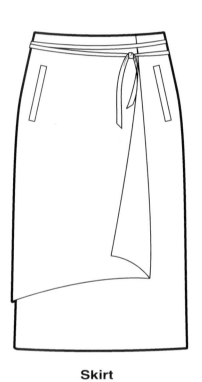

Skirt

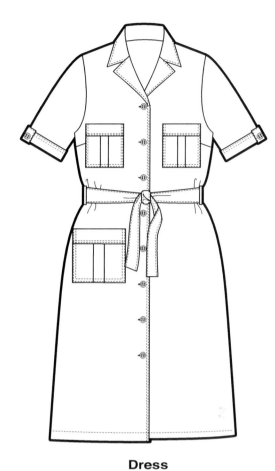

Dress

Outerwear

All flats are drawn on croquis figures at 75% scale.

Sweater

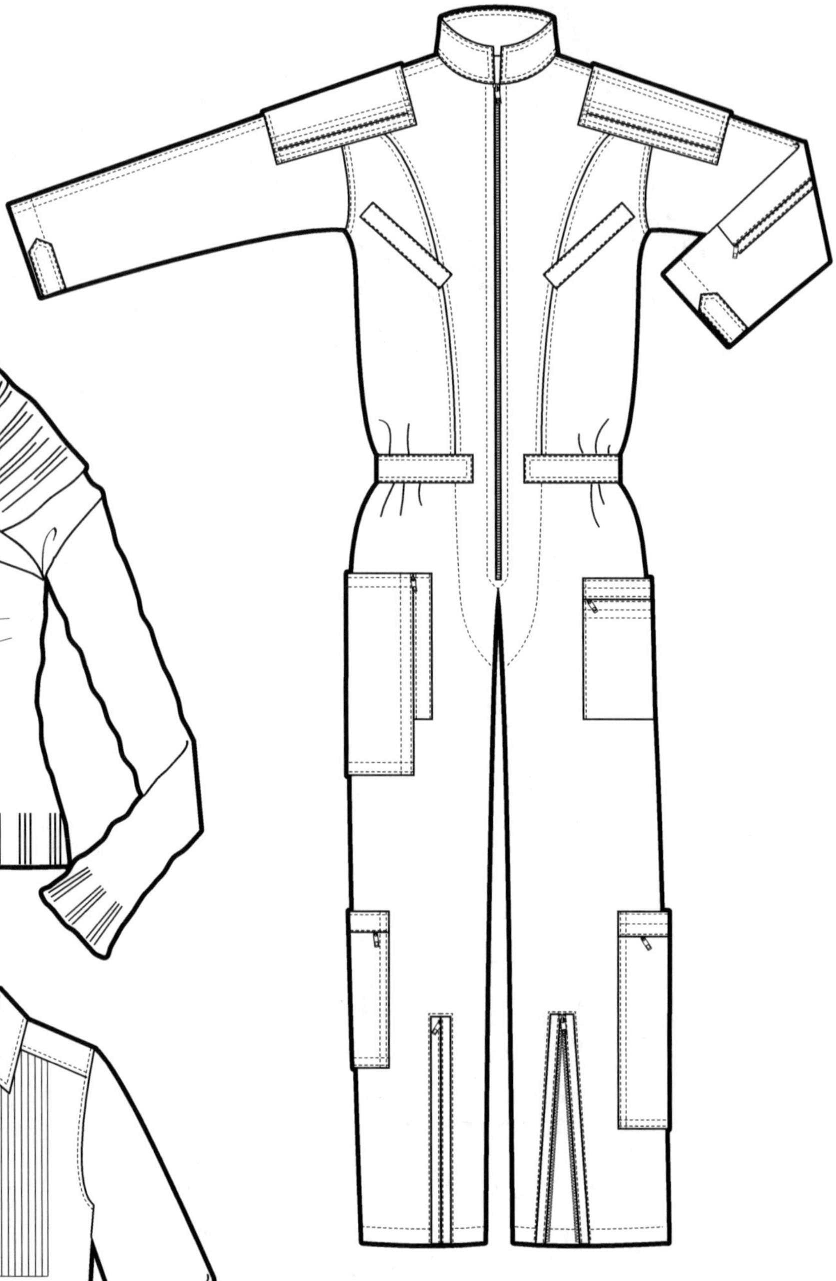

Woven Shirt

Jumpsuit

Tailored Jacket

Vest

Outerwear

Skirt

Pants

Dress

All flats are drawn on croquis figures at 75% scale.

14

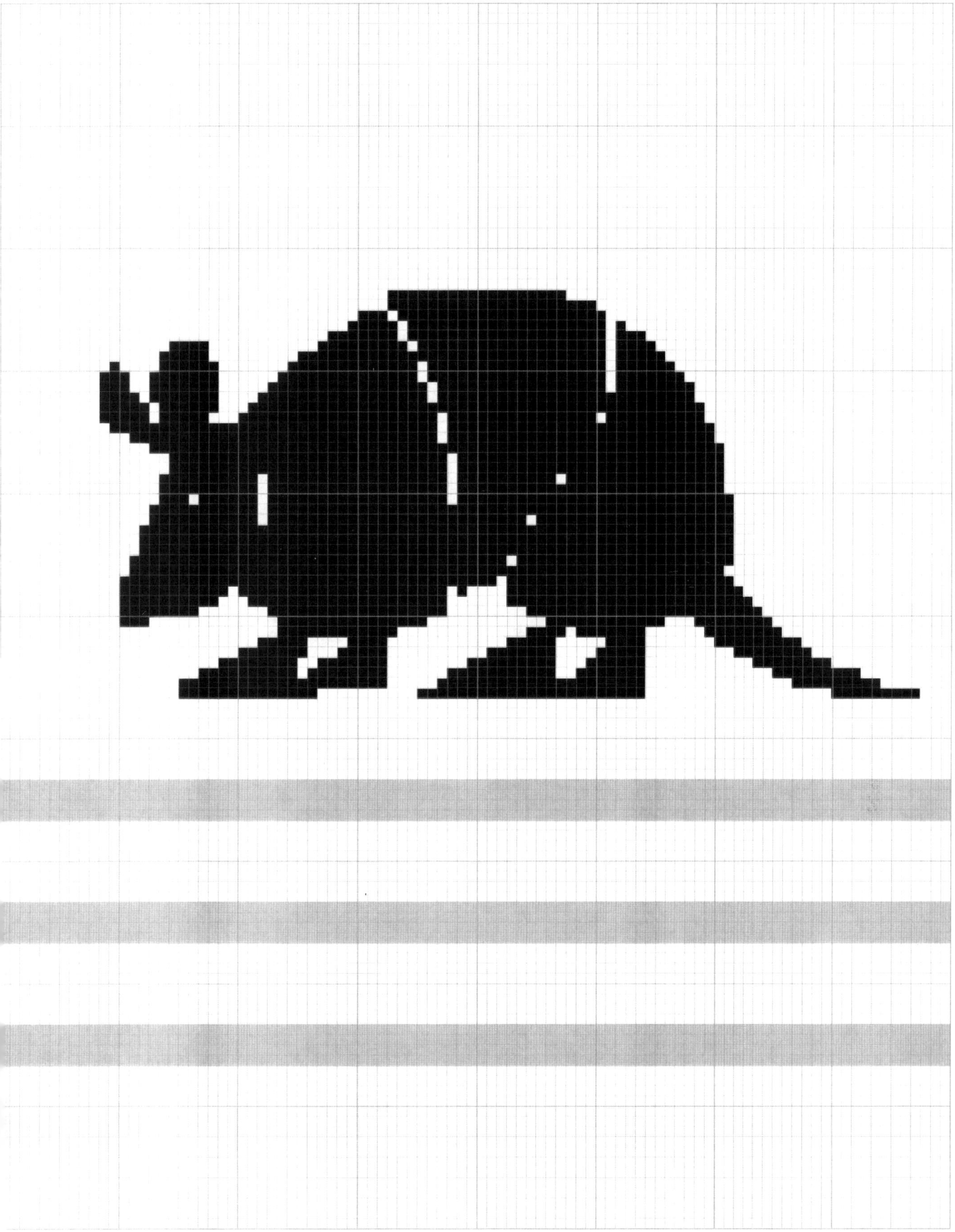

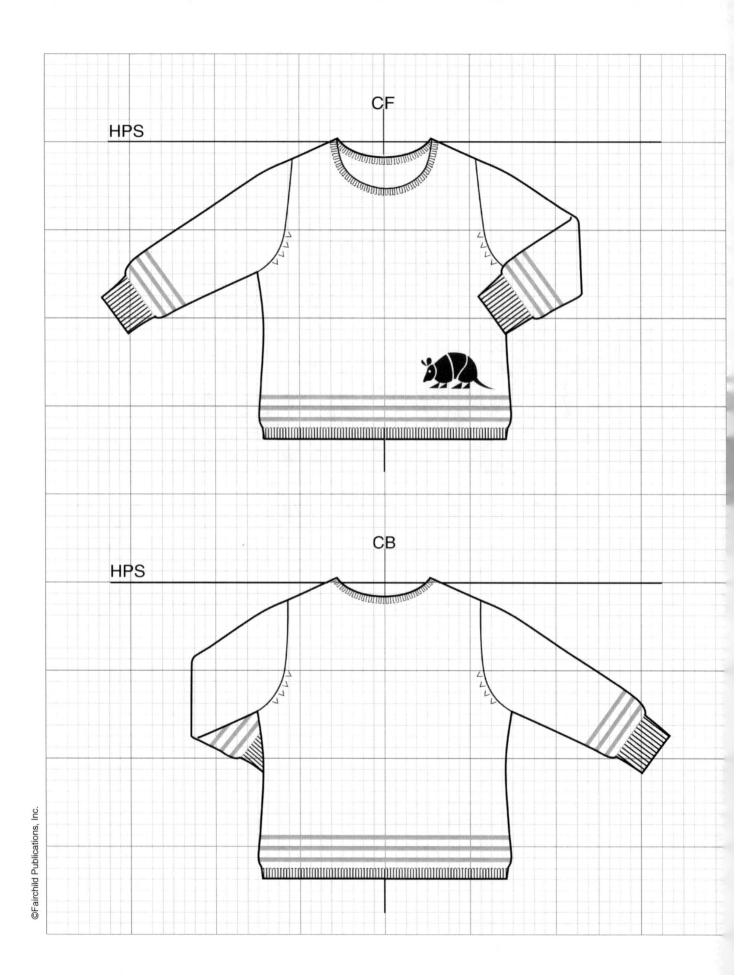

CF

CB

HPS

SAMPLE SPEC SHEETS AND GARMENT GRAPHS

Sweater Spec Sheet

NAME:			DATE:			
SEASON:	**FALL**	STYLE: **f130629V0**	SIZE:	**PLUS 1W**		
DESCRIPTION:	**TUNIC WITH SCOOP NECK, 3/4 L, SLEEVES, RIB TRIM, HORIZONTAL STRIPE PATTERN**					
	WITH ARMADILLO INTARSIA					
FABRICATION:	**100% COTTON**					
ACCESSORIES:			TRIM:	**3" CUFF, 1" BODY TRIM, .5" NECK TRIM**		
KNIT STITCHES:	**TRIM 1X1 RIB, FULL NEEDLE RIB BODY, 3" FEEDER STRIPE PATTERN, BODY & SLEEVE 12-14 GAUGE**					

		FRONT	BACK	TOTAL	COMMENTS
1	NECK DROP	4.50	2.00		
2	NECK – WIDTH	8.50			
3	NECK CIRCUMFERENCE				
	a. Relaxed	14.00	10.00		
	b. Extended	15.00	10.50		
4	COLLAR HEIGHT / RIB TRIM @ CF/CB	0.50	0.50		
5	NECK OPENING AT TOP OF TRIM				
	a. Relaxed	14.00	10.00		
	b. Extended	15.00	10.50		
6	SHOULDER – LENGTH	5.50			
7	ACROSS SHOULDER	17.00	18.00		
8	SHOULDER SLOPE FROM HPS	2.00			
9	LENGTH *				
	a. HPS	27.00	27.00		
	b. CF/CB	22.50	25.00		
	c. Side	15.25			
10	HPS TO UNDERARM	11.75	12.00		
11	ARMHOLE CIRCUMFERENCE	10.50	10.50	21.00	
12	RAGLAN SEAM				
13	ACROSS CHEST	23.00	23.50	46.50	
14	WAIST MEASURE FROM HPS	17.00	17.00		
15	ACROSS WAIST	22.50	22.50	45.00	
16	SWEEP				
	a. Relaxed	22.50	23.00	45.50	
	b. Extended	25.50	26.00	51.50	
17	BODY WIDTH AT TRANSFER POINT	23.00	23.50	46.50	
18	SLEEVE - LENGTH / Set-In *				
	a. Overarm	20.00			
	b. Underarm	15.00			
	c. CB		29.75		
	d. HPS		25.50		
19	SLEEVE - LENGTH / Raglan *				
	a. Overarm				
	b. Underarm				
	c. CB				
20	UPPER SLEEVE – WIDTH	7.00	7.00	14.00	
21	ELBOW	6.00	6.00	12.00	
22	CUFF WIDTH AT TRANSFER POINT	5.00	5.00	10.00	
23	CUFF OPENING				
	a. Relaxed	4.50	4.50	9.00	
	b. Extended	6.00	6.00	12.00	
24	CUFF TRIM – HEIGHT	3.00	3.00		
25	BODY TRIM – HEIGHT	1.00	1.00		
26	FRONT PLACKET				
	a. Length				
	b. Width				
27	POCKET A				
	a. Placement - distance from HPS				
	b. Placement - distance from CF				
	c. Pocket Width				
	d. Pocket Length				
28	POCKET B				
	a. Placement - distance from HPS				
	b. Placement - distance from CF				
	c. Pocket Width				
	d. Pocket Length				
29	BUTTON PLACEMENT	N/A			

REMARKS/OTHER SPECS: All measurements in inches; all graphs drawn at .125" = 1" scale

* Circle method for measuring   Abbreviations: high point of shoulder (HPS), center front (CF), center back (CB)

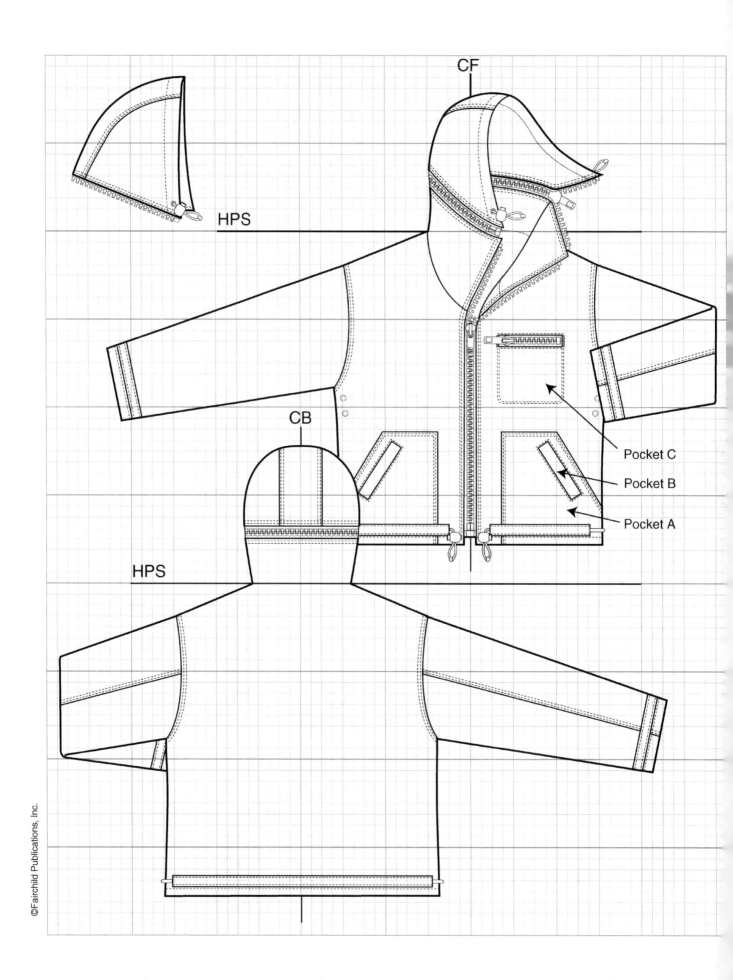

CF

HPS

CB

HPS

Pocket C

Pocket B

Pocket A

SAMPLE SPEC SHEETS AND GARMENT GRAPHS

Outerwear Spec Sheet

NAME:			DATE:			
SEASON: **FALL**		STYLE: **P9706**	SIZE: **LARGE**			
DESCRIPTION: ZIP OFF HOOD JACKET W/EXPOSED CF ZIPPER, 2 ANGLED WELT POCKETS, 2 PATCH POCKETS,						
ZIPPER ENTRY POCKET AND DRAWSTRING SWEEP						
FABRICATION/SHELL: **VINYL**		BACKING: **POLYESTER**		LINING: **190T NYLON**		
TRIM: 1.25" REFLECTIVE TAPE, 4 SIZE10mm x 18 METAL GROMMETS SILVER DULL FINISH						
SNAPS: **NA**			CORDLOCKS: **ROUND METAL STOPPERS SILVER DULL FINISH**			
ZIPPER: **#5YKK METAL SILVER DULL FINISH**			DRAWSTRING: **Cotton to match shell color/size 5mm**			

		FRONT	BACK	TOTAL	COMMENTS
1	NECK DROP	7.00	0.00		
2	NECK – WIDTH	7.50			
3	NECK CIRCUMFERENCE	16.50	8.75	25.25	
4	COLLAR				
	a. Width @ CB		4.00		
	b. Width @ point	6.75			
	c. Spread				
5	SHOULDER – LENGTH	8.50			
6	ACROSS SHOULDER	23.25			
7	LENGTH*				
	a. HPS	28.50	28.50		
	b. CF/CB	21.50	28.50		
	c. Side	15.25	15.25		
8	ACROSS CHEST	25.75	26.00	51.75	
9	HPS TO WAIST	18.50	18.50		
10	ACROSS WAIST	25.25	26.00	51.25	
11	BOTTOM EDGE OPENING (SWEEP)				
	a. Relaxed				
	b. Extended	25.00	26.00	51.00	
12	HPS TO UNDERARM	15.00	15.00		
13	HPS TO SLEEVE SEAM		8.25		
14	ARMHOLE CIRCUMFERENCE	12.50	12.50	25.00	
15	SLEEVE – LENGTH *				
	a. Overarm	23.50			
	b. Underarm	20.00			
	c. CB		35.50		
	d. HPS		32.50		
16	UPPER SLEEVE – WIDTH @ FOLD	10.75	10.75	21.50	
17	ELBOW @ FOLD	9.00	9.00	18.00	
18	SLEEVE CUFF OPENING				
	a. Relaxed				
	b. Extended		13.50		
19	CUFF – HEIGHT				
20	FRONT PLACKET – LENGTH				
21	FRONT PLACKET – WIDTH				
22	POCKET A				
	a. Placement – HPS to top pocket edge	18.25			
	b. Placement – CF to pocket edge (top/bottom)	3.00			
	c. Placement – Side seam to pocket edge (top/bottom)	4.00			
	d. Pocket width (top/bottom)	5.5, 9.25			
	e. Pocket length	4.00,10.25			
23	POCKET B				
	a. Placement – HPS to top pocket edge	19.00			
	b. Placement – CF to pocket edge (top/bottom)	7.25, 10.25			
	c. Placement – Side seam to pocket edge (top/bottom)	4.75, 1.75			
	d. Pocket width	1.00			
	e. Pocket length	5.75			
24	POCKET C				
	a. Placement – HPS to top pocket edge	9.50			
	b. Placement – CF to pocket edge (top/bottom)	2.50			
	c. Placement – Side seam to pocket edge (top/bottom)	3.75			
	d. Pocket width	6.00			
	e. Pocket length	6.50			
25	HPS TO YOKE				
26	HOOD				
	a. Height	12.50			
	b. Depth			10.25	
	c. Center panel	4.00	4.00		
27	DRAWCORD TUNNEL				
	a. Hood			1.00	
	b. Sweep	1.00	1.00		

REMARKS/OTHER SPECS: All measurements in inches; all graphs drawn at .125" = 1" scale
   SHOULDER SLOPE HPS TO ARMHOLE 3"
* Circle method for measuring   Abbreviations: high point of shoulder (HPS), center front (CF), center back (CB)

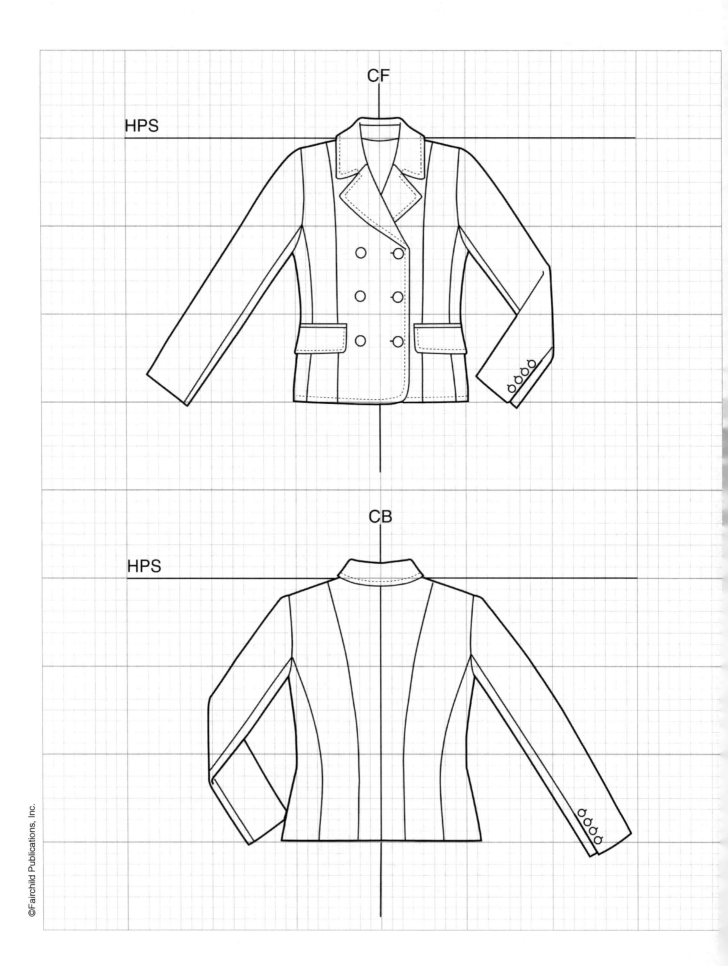

CF

CB

HPS

SAMPLE SPEC SHEETS AND GARMENT GRAPHS

Tailored Jacket Spec Sheet

NAME:		DATE:		
SEASON: **FALL**	STYLE:	SIZE: **4**		

DESCRIPTION: TAILORED SHAPED JACKET WITH NOTCHED SHAWL COLLAR, DOUBLE BREASTED CLOSURE, FLAP POCKETS, AND VENTED SLEEVES

FABRICATION: 94% WOOL, 5% CASHMERE, 1% ELASTENE, FUSIBLE & POLYESTER LINING

ACCESSORIES: TRIM:

		FRONT	BACK	TOTAL	COMMENTS
1	NECK DROP	5.25	0.25		
2	NECK – WIDTH	6.00			
3	SHOULDER – LENGTH	5.50			
4	ACROSS SHOULDER	15.00	15.50	15.00	
5	ACROSS BACK		15.00		
6	LENGTH *				
	a. From HPS	24.00	24.00		
	b. @ CF/CB	18.75	23.75		
	c. Side	14.50			
7	HPS TO UNDERARM	9.50	9.00		
8	ACROSS CHEST	16.50	16.50	33.00	
9	HPS TO WAIST	17.00	17.00		
10	HALF WAIST	18.00			
11	BOTTOM EDGE OPENING (sweep)	18.00	19.00	37.00	PLUS 5" OVERLAP
12	ARMHOLE CIRCUMFERENCE	9.50	9.00	18.50	
13	PRINCESS SEAM PLACEMENT				
	a. From HPS	2.00	2.00		
	b. From CF/CB @ armhole (or shoulder seam)	4.25	3.00		
	c. From CF/CB @ waist	4.00	1.50		
	d. From CF/CB @ sweep	4.25	2.00		
14	SIDE PANEL WIDTH				
	a. Armhole	2.00	2.00		
	b. Waist	3.00	2.50		
	c. Sweep	4.00	3.50		
15	COLLAR WIDTH				
	a. @ CENTER BACK		2.50		
	b @ POINT	2.50			
16	LAPEL WIDTH @ POINT	3.50			
17	SLEEVE – LENGTH *				
	a. Overarm			25.00	
	b. Underarm			18.00	
	c. CB			33.50	
	d. HPS			30.50	
18	UPPER SLEEVE WIDTH	6.00	6.00	12.00	
19	ELBOW	5.50	5.50	11.00	
20	SLEEVE OPENING	5.00	5.00	5.00	
21	SLEEVE VENT – LENGTH			5.00	
22	SLEEVE PANEL FOR TWO PIECE SLEEVE			4.50	
23	DEPTH OF SLEEVE HEM	1.375	1.375		
24	POCKET A				
	a. Placement – Distance from HPS	17			
	b. Placement – Distance From CF	2.625			
	c. Pocket width	.25			
	d. Pocket length	5.25			
	e. Pocket flap width	2.25			
	f. Pocket flap length	5.25			
25	POCKET B				
	a. Placement – Distance from HPS				
	b. Placement – Distance From CF				
	c. Pocket width				
	d. Pocket length				
	e. Pocket flap width				
	f. Pocket flap length				
26	POCKET C				
	a. Placement – Distance from HPS				
	b. Placement – Distance From CF				
	c. Pocket width				
	d. Pocket length				
	e. Pocket flap width				
	f. Pocket flap length				
27	BINDING – WIDTH/HEM	1.25			
28	BUTTON PLACEMENT - 1st BUTTON 9.25, 2nd BUTTON 3.75, 3rd BUTTON 3.75				

REMARKS/OTHER SPECS: All measurements in inches; all graphs drawn at .125" = 1" scale

STITCH: SN .25" FROM EDGE - AROUND COLLAR, LAPEL, FRONT, HEM, POCKET FLAPS

* Circle method for measuring   Abbreviations: high point of shoulder (HPS), center front (CF), center back (CB)

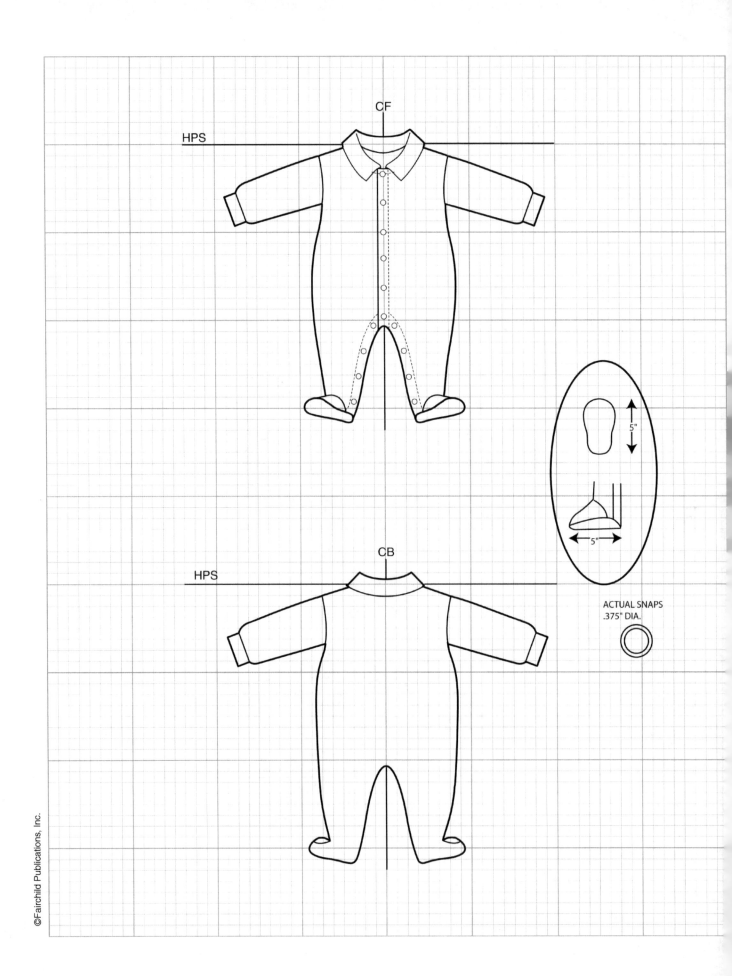

CF

HPS

CB

HPS

5"

5"

ACTUAL SNAPS
.375" DIA.

SAMPLE SPEC SHEETS AND GARMENT GRAPHS

Bodysuits and Jumpsuits Spec Sheet

NAME:			DATE:			
SEASON: FALL		STYLE:	SIZE: 12 MONTHS			
DESCRIPTION: 1 PIECE BOY'S SLEEPSUIT W/CF SNAP CLOSURE, ROLL COLLAR, ATTACHED FEET, SLEEVE CUFF						
FABRICATION: 75% COTTON, 25% POLYESTER						
ACCESSORIES:			TRIM: 15 SNAPS - SIZE 1			

		FRONT	BACK	TOTAL	COMMENTS
1	NECK DROP	1.50	0.75		
2	NECK – WIDTH	4.75			
3	NECK CIRCUMFERENCE	6.50	4.50	11.00	ADD 1" OVERLAP
4	SHOULDER – LENGTH	3.00			
5	ACROSS SHOULDER	12.00			
6	TORSO – LENGTH *				
	a. HPS to crotch relaxed	16.50	16.50		
	b. HPS to crotch extended	17.50	17.50		
	c. CF/CB length relaxed	14.25	15.75		
	d. CF/CB length extended	15.25	16.75		
7	ACROSS BACK		11.00		
8	HPS TO UNDERARM	5.50			
9	ACROSS CHEST	11.50	11.50	23.00	
10	HPS TO WAIST	8.00	8.00		
11	ACROSS WAIST				
	a. Relaxed	12.00	12.75	24.75	CF NECKLINE TO W 6.25"
	b. Extended	13.00	13.75	26.75	
12	HIGH HIP	13.75	13.75	27.50	3" FROM WAIST
13	LOW HIP	13.00	13.50	26.50	5" FROM WAIST
14	LEG OPENING				
	a. relaxed				
	b. extended				
15	CROTCH – WIDTH				
16	RISE	8.50	8.50		
17	ARMHOLE CIRCUMFERENCE	5.50	5.50	11.00	
18	UPPER SLEEVE – WIDTH	4.50	4.50	9.00	
19	ELBOW	4.00	4.00	8.00	
20	SLEEVE – LENGTH *				
	a. Overarm	9.50			
	b. Underarm	8.50			
	c. CB		15.00		
	d. HPS		12.50		
21	CUFF/SLEEVE BOTTOM				
	a. Relaxed	3.00	3.00	6.00	
	b. Extended	3.50	3.50	7.00	
	c. Width			1.00	
22	CB LENGTH TO LEG BOTTOM				
	a. Relaxed		23.25		
	b. Extended		25.00		
23	INSEAM	9.00			
24	THIGH CIRCUMFERENCE	5.25	5.25	10.50	
25	KNEE CIRCUMFERENCE	4.00	4.00	8.00	
26	BOTTOM OPENING	3.25	3.25	6.50	
27	COLLAR				
	a. Width - CB		2.25		
	b. Width @ point	2.25			
	c. Spread	3.25			
28	PLACKET				
	a. Width				
	b. Length				
29	POCKET				
	a. Placement – Distance from HPS				
	b. Placement – Distance From CF				
	c. Pocket width				
	d. Pocket length				
	e. Pocket flap width				
30	BUTTON PLACEMENT - SNAPS .5" TO 1st, 2.25" to SNAPS 2-6 / SNAPS INSEAM 1" TO 1st, 2.25" TO SNAPS 2-4				

REMARKS/OTHER SPECS/STITCHING: All measurements in inches; all graphs drawn at .125" = 1" scale

  STITCH - SN - .75" FROM INSEAM, 1" FROM FRONT CLOSURE, .25" NECK CIRCUMFERENCE

  FOOT ATTACH - SOLE 5" L, TOP OF FOOT - 3" W / 3" L

* Circle method for measuring   Abbreviations: high point of shoulder (HPS), center front (CF), center back (CB), single needle (SN)

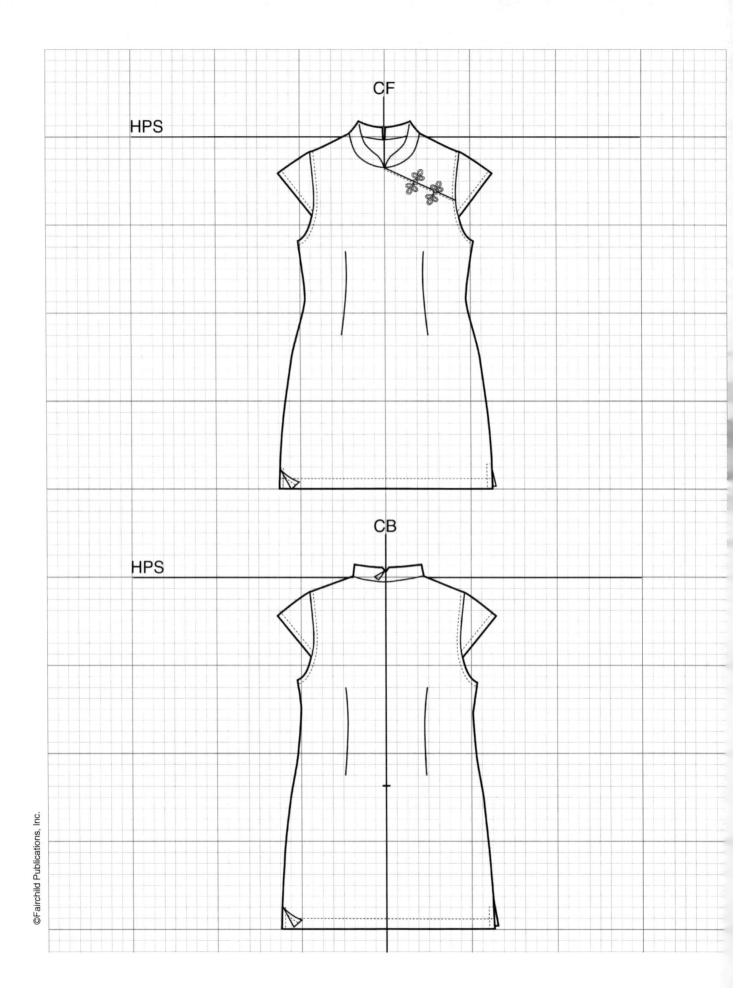

CF

Dress Spec Sheet

NAME:			DATE:			
SEASON: SPRING		STYLE: CHEONG SAM	SIZE:	14 PRETEEN		
DESCRIPTION: MANDARIN COLLAR, CAP SLEEVES, FRONT FROG DETAILS AND BACK ZIPPER CLOSURE						
FABRICATION: 97% POLYESTER, 3% SPANDEX						
ACCESSORIES:		TRIM: 1-19" INVISIBLE ZIPER, 2 FROGS W/ 15 LIGHE KNOTTED BUTTONS				

		FRONT	BACK	TOTAL	COMMENTS
1	NECK DROP	2.75	0.25		
2	NECK – WIDTH	7.00			
3	NECK CIRCUMFERENCE	9.00	8.00	17.00	
4	SHOULDER – LENGTH	4.00			
5	ACROSS SHOULDER			14.50	
6	LENGTH *				
	a. HPS	32.00	32.00		
	b. CF/CB	29.25	31.75		
	c. Side			23.50	
7	ACROSS BACK		14.00		4" FROM CB
8	ACROSS CHEST	16.50	16.50	33.00	
9	WAIST – LENGTH *				
	a. CF/CB	11.25	13.75		
	b. HPS	14.00	14.00		
10	ACROSS WAIST				
	a. Relaxed	15.50	16.00	31.50	
	b. Extended				
11	HIGH HIP	16.00	16.50	32.50	3" FROM WAIST
12	LOW HIP	17.50	18.00	35.50	6" FROM WAIST
13	BOTTOM EDGE OPENING (SWEEP)	20.00	20.00	40.00	
14	HPS TO UNDERARM	9.50			
15	ARMHOLE CIRCUMFERENCE	8.50	9.50	18.00	
16	UPPER SLEEVE – WIDTH				
17	SLEEVE – LENGTH *				
	a. Overarm	3.50			
	b. Underarm				
	c. CB		11.00		
	d. HPS		7.50		
18	ELBOW				
19	SLEEVE HEM/CUFF OPENING				
	a. Relaxed	5.00	4.00	9.00	
	b. Extended				
20	DEPTH OF SLEEVE HEM			0.25	
21	CUFF HEIGHT				
22	DART				
	a. Placement – CF/CB to top of dart	3.50	3.50		
	b. Placement – HPS to top of dart	10.50	10.00		
	c. Placement – CF/CB to bottom of dart	3.50	3.75		
	d. Placement – HPS to bottom of dart	18.00	18.00		
	e. Dart – Length	7.50	8.00		
23	BINDING WIDTH/HEM			1.00	
24	BUTTON PLACEMENT	SEE FROGS			

REMARKS/OTHER SPECS/STITCHING: All measurements in inches; all graphs drawn at .125" = 1" scale

COLLAR STAND - FRONT/BACK 1"

YOKE SEAM - LEFT SIDE ONLY
  CF TO ARMHOLE L - 6.5"
  HPS TO YOKE TOP 3.25"
  HPS TO YOKE BOTTOM 5.5"

SIDE SLITS 2"

2 FROGS
  L - 2.25"
  W - .875"

FROG 'A'
CF TO TOP - .75
CF TO BOTTOM 2"
HPS TO TOP 3"
HPS TO BOTTOM 5.25

FROG 'B'
CF TO TOP 4.75"
CF TO BOTTOM 3.75"
HPS TO TOP 4"
HPS TO BOTTOM 6.25"

STITCH - SN .25" FROM EDGE -
ARMHOLE SLEEVE HEM,
SIDE SLIT

SN AT EDGE - YOKE

SN - HEM

BAR TAC - TOP OF SLIT

Circle method for measuring

Abbreviations: high point of shoulder (HPS), center front (CF), center back (CB), single needle (SN)

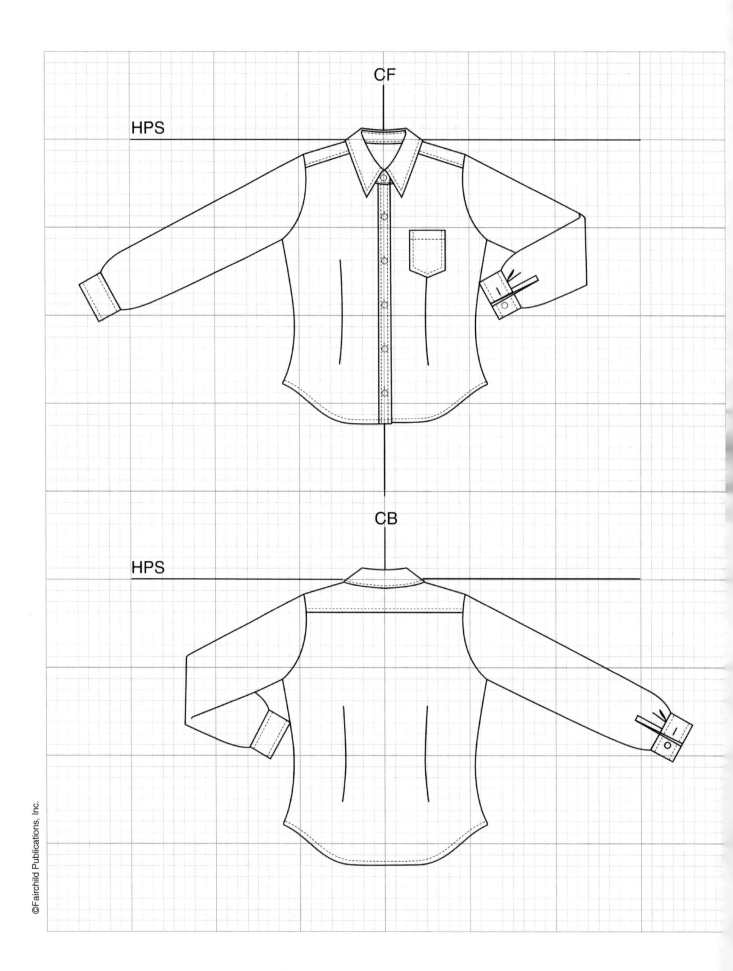

CF

HPS

CB

HPS

SAMPLE SPEC SHEETS AND GARMENT GRAPHS

Woven Shirt Spec Sheet

NAME:			DATE:		
SEASON: FALL		STYLE:	SIZE: MISSY MEDUIM		
DESCRIPTION: SEMI-FITTED SHIRT, ROLL COLLAR W/STAND, LONG SLEEVE BUTTON THROUGH CUFF,					
FRONT PLACKET CLOSURE					
FABRICATION: 60% COTTON, 35% POLYESTER, 5% SPANDEX					
ACCESSORIES:			TRIM:	8-19 LIGNE BUTTONS	

		FRONT	BACK	TOTAL	COMMENTS
1	NECK DROP	4.00	0.50		
2	NECK – WIDTH	6.00			
3	SHOULDER – LENGTH	5.00			
4	ACROSS SHOULDER			15.25	
5	LENGTH *				
	a. HPS	26.00	26.00		
	b. CF/CB	22.00	25.50		
	c. Side	13.75	13.75		
6	HPS TO UNDERARM	9.50			
7	ACROSS CHEST	19.00	19.00	38.00	
8	ACROSS WAIST	17.00	17.00	34.00	
9	BOTTOM EDGE OPENING (Sweep)	19.00	19.00	38.00	ADD 1" FOR OVERLAP
10	COLLAR BAND				
	a. Height		1.25		
	b. Length			15.75	
11	COLLAR				
	a. Width - center back		2.00		
	b. Width @ point	3.00			
	c. Spread	3.50			
12	ARMHOLE CIRCUMFERENCE	9.75	9.00	18.75	
13	UPPER SLEEVE – WIDTH	6.50	6.50	13.00	
14	SLEEVE – LENGTH *				
	a. Overarm	24.50			
	b. Underarm	18.50			
	c. CB		32.50		
	d. HPS		25.50		
15	ELBOW	6.00	6.00	12.00	
16	SLEEVE OPENING	5.00	5.00	10.00	
17	CUFF – HEIGHT			2.50	
18	CUFF OPENING	4.00	4.00	8.00	.25" OVERLAP - BUTTONED
19	SLEEVE PLACKET				
	a. Length	3.00			
	b. Width	0.75			
20	DEPTH OF SLEEVE HEM				
21	BINDING – WIDTH/HEM			0.25	
22	FRONT PLACKET – WIDTH	1.00			
23	YOKE	1.25	3.00		
24	POCKET				
	a. Placement – Distance from HPS	8.25			
	b. Placement – Distance From CF	2.50			
	c. Pocket width	3.50			
	d. Pocket length	4.00			
	e. Pocket flap width				
	f. Pocket flap length				
25	PLEATS				
	a. Placement - distance from CF/CB	0.75			PLACEMENT FROM SLEEVE OPENING
	b. Depth	0.50			
26	DART				
	a. Placement HPS	11.50	11.50		
	b. Placement CF/CB	3.50	3.50		
	c. Length	9.00	9.00		
27	BUTTON PLACEMENT 1st .5", 2-5 3.5" APART				

REMARKS/OTHER SPECS: All measurements in inches; all graphs drawn at .125" = 1" scale

STITCH - SN - .25" FROM EDGE-HEM, YOKE, PLACKET, CUFF, COLLAR

    SN - EDGE - POCKET

* Circle method for measuring   Abbreviations: high point of shoulder (HPS), center front (CF), center back (CB), single needle (SN)

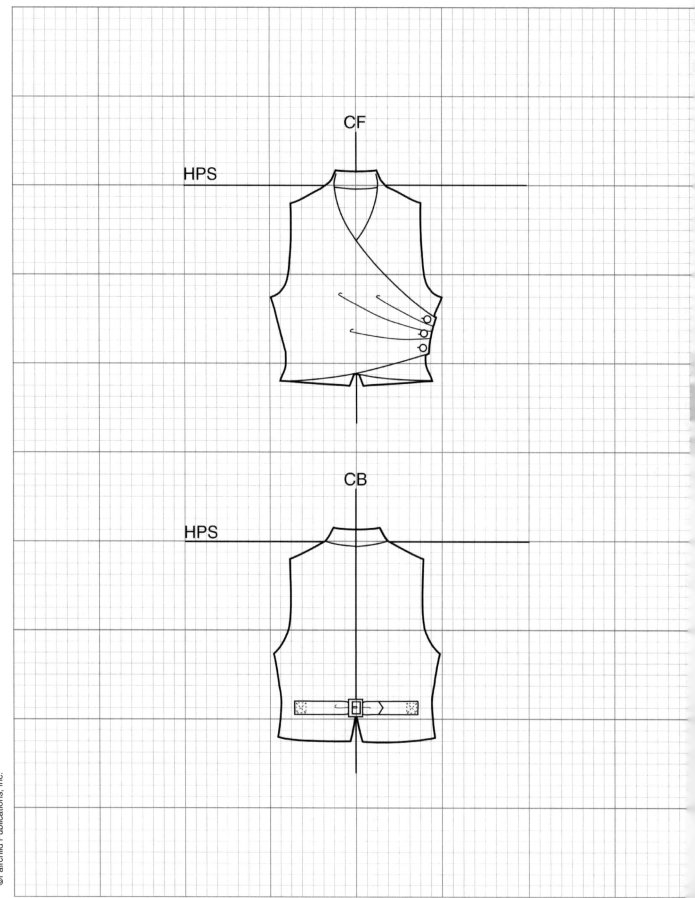

CF

HPS

CB

HPS

SAMPLE SPEC SHEETS AND GARMENT GRAPHS

Vest Spec Sheet

NAME:			DATE:			
SEASON: FALL		STYLE:	SIZE: 4 PETITE			
DESCRIPTION: ASSYMETRICAL PLEATED WRAP VEST WITH BUTTON CLOSURE AND BACK BELT DETAIL						
FABRICATION: 70% WOOL, 30% RAYON - FULLY LINED-RAYON						
ACCESSORIES:			TRIM: 6-27 LIGNE BUTTONS, 1" X 75" BUCKLE			

		FRONT	BACK	TOTAL	COMMENTS
1	NECK DROP	4.75	0.25		
2	NECK – WIDTH	3.00	6.00		
3	FRONT – OPENING	20.00			
4	SHOULDER – LENGTH	5.00			
5	ACROSS SHOULDER		12.00		
6	LENGTH*				
	a. CF	12.50			
	b. CB		17.75		
	c. HPS	17.25	18.00		
	d. Side			8.00	
7	HPS TO UNDERARM	10.00			
8	ARMHOLE	9.50	9.50	19.00	
9	ACROSS CHEST	15.00	15.00	30.00	
10	ACROSS WAIST	13.00	14.00	27.00	15" FROM HPS
11	POCKET A				
	a. Placement – Distance from HPS				
	b. Placement – Distance from CF				
	c. Width				
	d. Length				
12	POCKET B				
	a. Placement – Distance from HPS				
	b. Placement – Distance from CF				
	c. Width				
	d. Length				
13	DART				
	a. Placement – Distance from HPS				
	b. Placement – Distance from CF				
	c. Length				
14	BINDING – WIDTH/HEM				
15	BOTTOM EDGE OPENING (Sweep)	14.00	14.00	28.00	PLUS 13" FOR OVERLAP
16	BUTTON PLACEMENT 1st BUTTON .5", 2nd BUTTON 1.25", 3rd BUTTON 1.5"				

REMARKS/OTHER SPECS: All measurements in inches; all graphs drawn at .125" = 1" scale

CB NECK STAND RISE 1.25"

3 FRONT PLEATS BOTH SIDES OF FRONT CLOSURE
   L 2"
   DEPTH 1"

PLEAT PLACEMENT
   1st .75" FROM TOP EDGE
   2nd 1.5" FROM TOP EDGE
   3rd 2" FROM TOP EDGE

FRONT CLOSURE AT SS
   L .75"
   RISE FROM HEM 2:
   FROM HPS 13"

CB SLIT
   L 2"

ATTACHED BACK BELT
   W 1.25"
   L RIGHT SIDE 8.5"
   L LEFT SIDE 6.75"

PLACEMENT OF BELT
   FROM SS 1.5"
   FROM HPS 14.5"

STITCHES
   SN - TOP STITCH
      ATTACHES BACK BELT
      ATTACHES BUCKLE

* Circle method for measuring   Abbreviations: high point of shoulder (HPS), center front (CF), center back (CB), single needle (SN)

©Fairchild Publications, Inc.

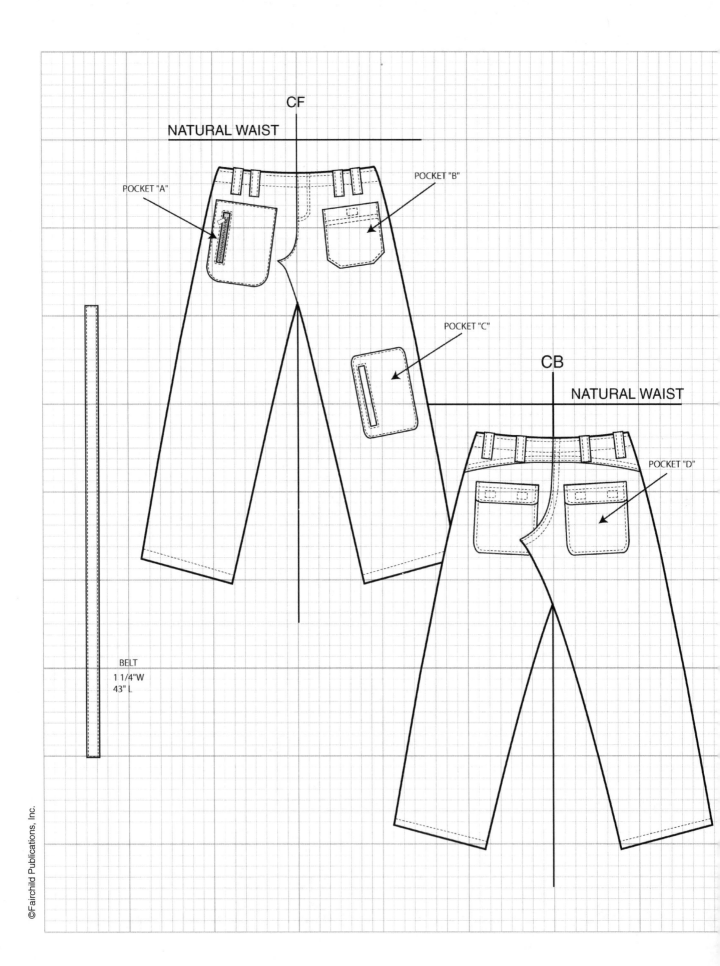

CF

NATURAL WAIST

POCKET "A"

POCKET "B"

POCKET "C"

CB

NATURAL WAIST

POCKET "D"

BELT
1 1/4"W
43" L

SAMPLE SPEC SHEETS AND GARMENT GRAPHS

Pants and Shorts Spec Sheet

SEASON: SPRING	STYLE: 2136	SIZE: JUNIOR 3		
DESCRIPTION: LOW RISE CARGO PANT WITH 5 POCKETS, CF ZIPPER ENTRY AND BACK YOKE				
FABRICATION: 100% COTTON RIP STOP				
ACCESSORIES: BELT-SAME FABRIC 1.25" X 43.00"		TRIM: 6.00", 4.50", AND 5.50" ZIPPER, 1.75" X 1" VELCRO		

		FRONT	BACK	TOTAL	COMMENTS
1	WAISTLINE SEAM PLACEMENT above/below natural waist*	4.50	4.50		
2	WAISTLINE SEAM CIRCUMFERENCE				
	a. Relaxed	15.50	14.00	29.50	ADD 1.50 FOR OVERLAP
	b. Extended				
3	WAISTBAND – HEIGHT			1.50	
4	HIGH HIP (4" from natural waist)	16.50	14.50	31.00	
5	LOW HIP (7" from natural waist)	17.50	16.50	34.00	
6	RISE	7.50	12.00		
7	INSEAM	32.00			
8	OUTSEAM	39.00			
9	THIGH CIRCUMFERENCE	10.25	12.50	22.75	
10	KNEE CIRCUMFERENCE	9.00	10.00	19.00	
11	ANKLE CIRCUMFERENCE	9.00	10.00	19.00	
12	ZIPPER PLACKET				
	a. Width	1.00			
	b. Length	4.50			
13	POCKET A				
	a. Placement – Waistline seam to top pocket edge	3.00			
	b. Placement – CF to pocket edge (top/bottom)	2.00			
	c. Placement – Side seam to pocket edge (top/bottom)	1.25			
	d. Placement – CB to pocket edge (top/bottom)				
	e. Pocket width	6.00			
	f. Pocket length	7.50			
14	POCKET B				
	a. Placement – Waistline seam to top pocket edge	3.00			
	b. Placement – CF to pocket edge (top/bottom)	2.50			
	c. Placement – Side seam to pocket edge (top/bottom)	1.25			
	d. Placement – CB to pocket edge (top/bottom)				
	e. Pocket width	5.00			
	f. Pocket length	5.00			
15	POCKET C				
	a. Placement – Waistline seam to top pocket edge	17.00			
	b. Placement – CF to pocket edge (top/bottom)				
	c. Placement – Side seam to pocket edge (top/bottom)	1.00			
	d. Placement – CB to pocket edge (top/bottom)				
	e. Pocket width	5.50			
	f. Pocket length	8.00			
16	POCKET D				
	a. Placement – Waistline seam to top pocket edge		4.50		
	b. Placement – CF to pocket edge (top/bottom)				
	c. Placement – Side seam to pocket edge (top/bottom)		2.00		
	d. Placement – CB to pocket edge (top/bottom)		1.00		
	e. Pocket width		6.00		
	f. Pocket length		7.00		
17	PLEAT				
	a. Placement – Distance from CF				
	b. Pleat depth				
18	BELT LOOP				
	a. Placement – Distance from CF	3.50			
	b. Distance from CB		2.50		
	c. Distance from SS	2.00	1.50		
	d. Belt loop width			0.75	
	e. Belt loop length			2.75	
19	DART				
	a. Placement – Distance from CF				
	b. Placement – Distance from CB				
	c. Dart length				
	d. Dart depth				
20	HEM – DEPTH			0.75	
21	CUFF – HEIGHT				
22	YOKE				
	a. Placement – Waistline seam to yoke @ CF/CB		2.50		
	b. Placement – Waistline seam to yoke @ SS		3.50		

REMARKS/OTHER SPECS: All measurements in inches; all graphs drawn at .125" = 1" scale

STITCH - SN EDGE ON WAIST, CF, POCKET EDGES, AND POCKET ZIPPERS/SN 1.50 BELOW WAIST TOP, .75 PANT HEM, .25 FROM EDGE ON BELT LOOPS, BELT, POCKET "B" TOP, AND POCKET "D" FLAP/DN ON BACK YOKE, CB SEAM AND FRONT ZIPPER PLACKET

* Circle method for measuring   Abbreviations: center front (CF), center back (CB), side seam (SS), single needle (SN), double needle (DN)

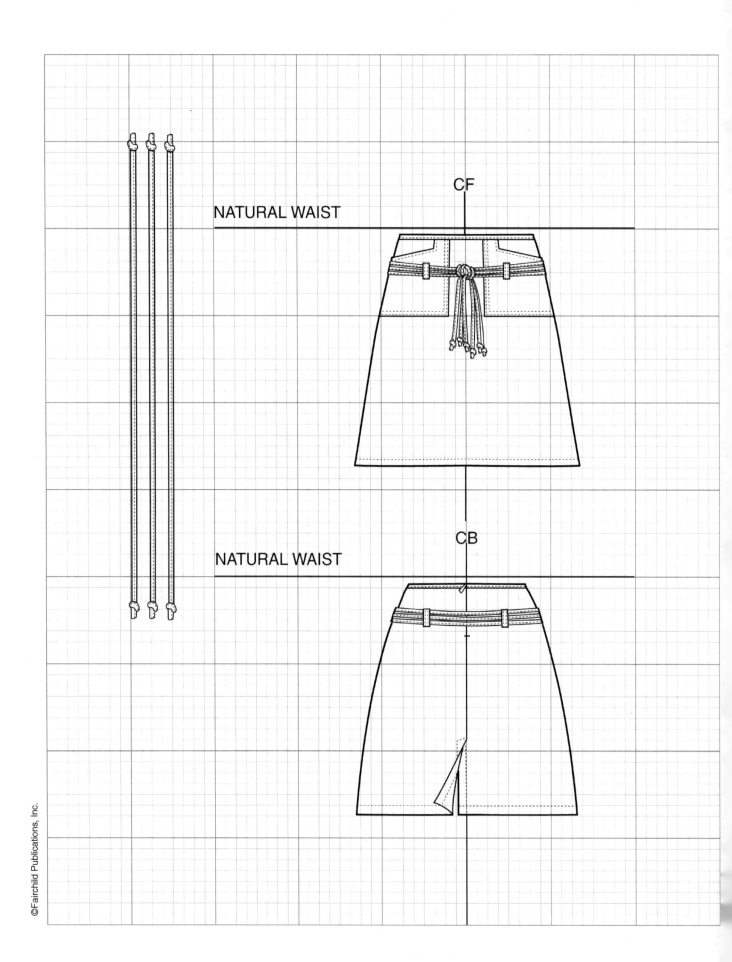

NATURAL WAIST

CF

CB

NATURAL WAIST

SAMPLE SPEC SHEETS AND GARMENT GRAPHS

Skirt Spec Sheet

NAME:			DATE:			
SEASON: **SUMMER**		STYLE: **2 - 3G06**	SIZE:	**12**		
DESCRIPTION: **PRE-TEEN DROPPED WAIST A-LINE WITH 2 FRONT PATCH POCKETS & 3 ATTACHED BIAS FABRIC BELTS**						

FABRICATION: **100% COTTON**						
ACCESSORIES:			TRIM: **5" ZIPPER, 3 BIAS BELTS .25" X 48"**			

		FRONT	BACK	TOTAL	COMMENTS
1	WAISTLINE SEAM PLACEMENT– above/below natural waist*	1.00	1.00		
2	WAISTLINE SEAM CIRCUMFERENCE				
	a. Relaxed	13.00	11.25	24.25	
	b. Extended				
3	WAISTBAND – HEIGHT	0.50	0.50		
4	HIGH HIP (4"-1"=3" from natural waist)	14.00	13.25	27.25	
5	LOW HIP (7"-1"=6" from natural waist)	15.00	14.50	29.50	
6	LENGTH				
	a. CF/CB	21.00	21.00		
	b. Side	21.00			
7	SWEEP	21.00	21.00	42.00	
8	SLIT				
	a. Length		7.00		
	b. Depth		0.75		
9	DART				
	a. Placement – CF/CB				
	b. Length				
	c. Depth				
10	POCKET A				
	a. Placement – Waist line seam to top pocket edge @ SS	1.75			
	b. Placement – CF to pocket edge	1.50, 3.00			
	c. Placement – Side seam to pocket edge (top/bottom)				
	d. Placement – CB to pocket edge (top/bottom)				
	e. Pocket width	6.50			
	f. Pocket length	7.00			
11	POCKET B				
	a. Placement – Waist line seam to top pocket edge				
	b. Placement – CF to pocket edge (top/bottom)				
	c. Placement – Side seam to pocket edge (top/bottom)				
	d. Placement – CB to pocket edge (top/bottom)				
	e. Pocket width				
	f. Pocket length				
12	PLEAT				
	a. Placement – Distance from CF				
	b. Depth				
13	ZIPPER PLACKET				
	a. Width (invisible zipper)				
	b. Length		5.00		
14	BELT LOOP				
	a. Placement – Distance from CF	3.75			
	b. Placement – Distance from CB		3.75		
	c. Placement – Distance from SS				
	d. Width	0.50	0.50		
	e. Length	2.25	2.25		
15	HEM – DEPTH	0.75	0.75		
16	BUTTON PLACEMENT	N/A			

REMARKS/OTHER SPECS: All measurements in inches; all graphs drawn at .125" = 1" scale

* Circle method for measuring   Abbreviations: high point of shoulder (HPS), center front (CF), center back (CB), side seam (SS)

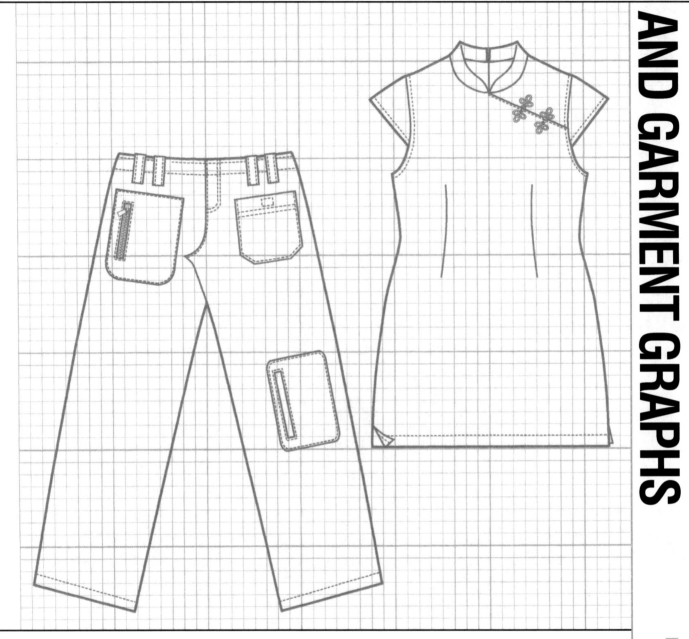

1 FRONT NECKLINE	Measure from center front to strap insertion. Include width of underwire and width of strap insertion. Multiply this measurement by two for both sides of neckline.
2 CENTER GORE	a. WIDTH @ GORE TOP – Measure from underwire seam across gore top to opposite underwire seam. b. HEIGHT – At center front measure from top to bottom of gore. c. WIDTH @ BOTTOM OF GORE – Measure from underwire seam across gore bottom to opposite underwire.
3 BRA BOTTOM LENGTH	a. CF TO CB – Measure at bra bottom from center front to center back. Multiply this measurement by two for total bra bottom length. b. CB TO HOOK EXTENSION – Measure from center back to end of hook extension. c. CB TO EYE EXTENSION – Measure from center back to end of eye extension.
4 BRA WIDTH	a. CF – TOP TO BOTTOM EDGE – Measure bra width at center front from bra top edge vertically down to bra hem. b. CENTER OF CUP BOTTOM TO HEM – Measure bra width below center of cup from underwire vertically down to bra hem. Do not include underwire. c. SIDE CUP SEAM TO HEM – Measure bra side width at side of underwire seam. Measure from bra top vertically down to bra hem. d. CB – TOP TO BOTTOM EDGE – Measure bra width at center back from bra top edge vertically down to bra hem edge.
5 BRA TOP	a. STRAP TO SIDE CUP – Measure bra top edge from strap insertion down side of cup to underwire seam. Include underwire. b. CUP TO CB – Measure bra top from underwire seam to center back. Do not include underwire. c. CB TO HOOK EXTENSION – Measure bra top from center back to end of hook extension. d. CB TO EYE EXTENSION – Measure bra top from center back to end of eye extension.
6 BRA CUP	a. TOP EDGE – Measure across top edge of bra cup from underwire to strap insertion. Include underwire width and strap Insertion width. b. SIDE – Measure across top side edge of bra cup from strap insertion to underwire. Include underwire. c. BOTTOM CIRCUMFERENCE – Measure underwire circumference from front to side. Measure at seam line. d. UNDERWIRE WIDTH – Measure width of underwire from seam to widest top stitch. e. HEIGHT @ PRINCESS LINE – Measure bra cup height at princess line from strap insertion vertically down to underwire. Include underwire.
7 SHOULDER STRAP – 2 in., or 5.08 cm, ADJUSTABLE LENGTH	a. FRONT INSERTION TO TOP EDGE OF FIRST ADJUSTABLE RING – Measure through center of strap. b. TOP EDGE OF FIRST ADJUSTABLE RING TO BACK INSERTION. c. WIDTH – Measure across width of strap from side edge to side edge.

©Fairchild Publications, Inc.

Illustrated Measurement Points for a Bra

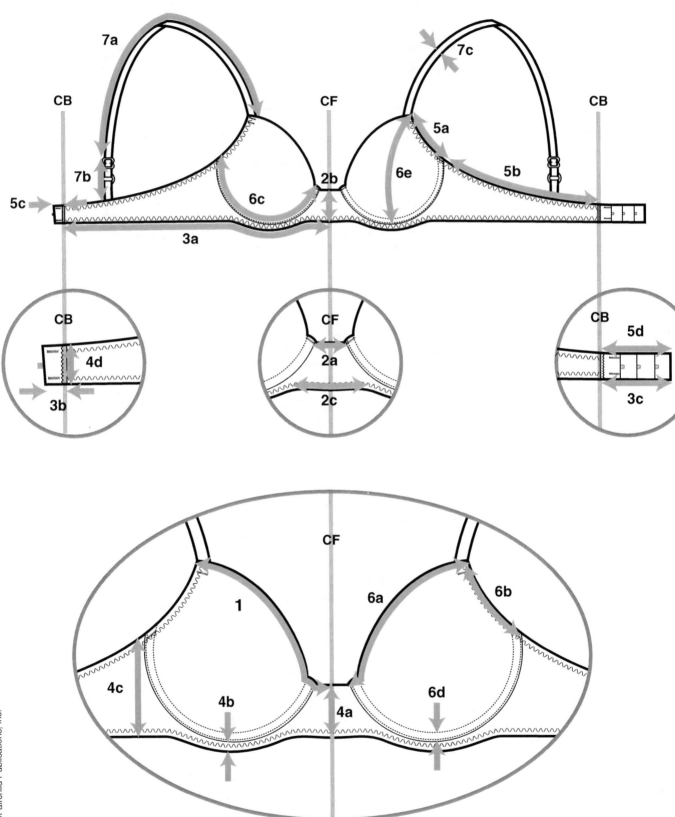

Bra Spec Sheet

NAME:			DATE:		
SEASON:	STYLE:		SIZE:	LABEL:	

DESCRIPTION:

FABRICATION:

ACCESSORIES: | | TRIM:

	FRONT	BACK	TOTAL	COMMENTS
1 FRONT NECKLINE – CF to strap				
2 CENTER GORE				
a. Width @ gore top				
b. Height				
c. Width @ bottom of gore				
3 BRA BOTTOM LENGTH				
a. CF to CB				
b. CB to hook extension				
c. CB to eye extension				
4 BRA WIDTH				
a. CF – Top to bottom edge				
b. Center of cup bottom to hem				
c. Side – Cup seam to hem				
d. CB – Top to bottom edge				
5 BRA TOP LENGTH				
a. Strap to side cup				
b. Cup to CB				
c. CB to hook extension				
d. CB to eye extension				
6 BRA CUP				
a. Top edge				
b. Side				
c. Bottom circumference				
d. Underwire width				
e. Height @ princess line				
7 SHOULDER STRAP – 2 in., or 5.08 cm, adjustable length				
a. Front insertion to top edge of first adjustable ring				
b. Top edge first adjustable ring to back insertion				
c. Width				

REMARKS/OTHER SPECS:

* Circle method for measuring   Abbreviations: high point of shoulder (HPS), center front (CF), center back (CB)

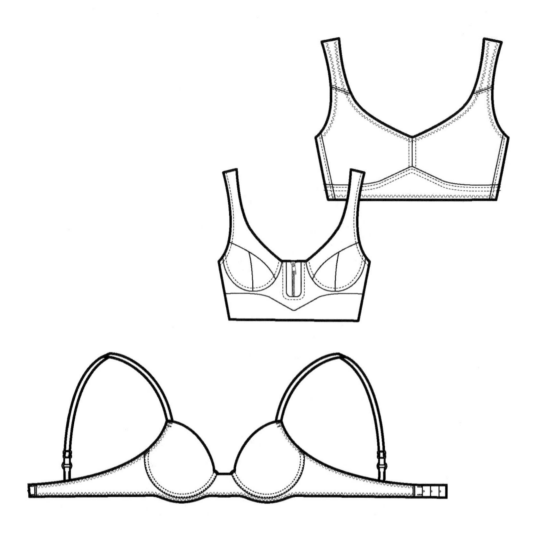

19 CUFF – HEIGHT	Measure straight down from top to bottom of cuff.	
20 FRONT PLACKET – LENGTH	Measure length of front placket vertically down center from top to the bottom.	
21 FRONT PLACKET – WIDTH	Measure across the placket.	
22 POCKET A	a. PLACEMENT – HPS to pocket edge – Measure vertically down from HPS to top edge of pocket.	
	b. PLACEMENT – CF to pocket edge [top/bottom] – Measure across from CF to edge of pocket.	
	c. PLACEMENT – Side seam to pocket edge [top/bottom] – Measure across from side seam to edge of pocket.	
	d. POCKET WIDTH – Measure across the top of the pocket.	
	e. POCKET LENGTH – Measure vertically down center of pocket from the top to the bottom. For irregularly shaped pockets, also measure down side edge.	
23 POCKET B	See #22	
24 POCKET FLAP	a. LENGTH – Measure down the center of the flap.	
	b. WIDTH – Measure across the top of the flap.	
25 HPS TO YOKE	a. FRONT – Measure down from the HPS line at shoulder to yoke seam.	
	b. BACK – Measure down from the HPS line at shoulder to yoke seam.	
26 HOOD	a. HEIGHT – Measure hood in a flattened position, following the hood opening edge from center front top fold down to neckline seam.	
	b. DEPTH – Measure hood in a flattened position at the widest point from the front edge to the center back fold.	
	c. CENTER PANEL – For three piece hood construction, measure width of center panel from seam to seam.	
27 DRAWCORD TUNNEL	a. HOOD – Measure width of casing for drawcord from outside edge of hood to casing stitch line.	
	b. SWEEP – Measure width of casing for drawcord from bottom edge to casing stitch line.	
28 BUTTON PLACEMENT	Measure the distance of the center of the first button to the neckline seam. Measure the distance of the center of the first button to the center of the second button. Typically, buttons are evenly spaced thereafter.	

Table of Measurement Points for Outerwear

#	Point	Description
1	NECK DROP	BACK – Some garments are designed with back necklines that scoop below the HPS. With the back of the garment facing you, measure at center back the distance of the back neckline from the HPS. FRONT – Measure down from the HPS line at center back to the neckline or collar seam at center front.
2	NECK – WIDTH	Measure straight across the neckline.
3	NECK CIRCUMFERENCE	With jacket open and laying flat, follow the contour of the neck seam total measurement inside the jacket from left CF to right CF.
4	COLLAR	a. WIDTH @ CB – Measure at center back from the collar seam to the edge of the collar. b. WIDTH @ POINT – Measure along the edge of the collar point. c. SPREAD – Measure across between the points of the collar.
5	SHOULDER – LENGTH	Measure along the shoulder seam from the neck seam to the armhole seam.
6	ACROSS SHOULDER	Measure from shoulder point (where the shoulder seam meets the armhole seam) to shoulder point.
7	LENGTH	There are several methods for measuring front length. Be sure to specify which of the following methods you use: a. HPS – Measure from the HPS straight down to the bottom of the garment. Measure both front and back lengths of garment. b. CF/CB – Measure down the center front of the garment from the neckline to the bottom. Measure down CB from neckline to bottom. c. SIDE – Measure the side seam from the armhole to the bottom of the garment. If the garment has slits, measure to where the slits begin.
8	ACROSS CHEST	Measure garment straight across one inch below armhole.
9	HPS TO WAIST	Measure down 17 in., or 43.18 cm, from the HPS to locate women's waistline. Drop 18 in., or 45.72 cm, for men's waist.
10	ACROSS WAIST	Locate waist from HPS, then measure horizontally across waist from side to side both front and back.
11	BOTTOM EDGE OPENING (SWEEP)	Making sure that garment is fully extended and following the contour of the hem, measure the bottom edge of the garment. a. RELAXED – Measure straight across bottom of jacket from side seam to side seam. b. EXTENDED – Measure as above with bottom edge fully extended.
12	HPS TO UNDERARM	Measure from the HPS line to the bottom of the armhole.
13	HPS TO SLEEVE SEAM	For a two piece sleeve, measure garment back. Measure from HPS line down armhole midway to seam insertion point.
14	ARMHOLE CIRCUMFERENCE	Following the armhole seam contour, measure from the shoulder point to the bottom of the armhole; the sum of the front and back measurements equal the total circumference.
15	SLEEVE – LENGTH	There are several methods for measuring sleeve length. Be sure to specify which of the following you use: a. OVERARM – Following the contour of the outside of the sleeve, measure from top of the armhole seam at shoulder to the bottom of the sleeve (including the cuff). b. UNDERARM – Measure from where the armhole and underarm seam meet to bottom of the sleeve (including the cuff). c. CB – With the back of the garment facing you, follow the contour of the sleeve and measure from the center back of the neckline to the bottom of the sleeve (including the cuff). Use this method for measuring sleeves with raglan armholes. d. HPS – Following the contour of the sleeve, measure from the HPS to the bottom of the sleeve (including the cuff).
16	UPPER SLEEVE – WIDTH	Measure straight across 1 in., or 2.54 cm, down from the armhole at a right angle to the folded edge of the sleeve; measure both front and back for total width.
17	ELBOW	Measure across midpoint of sleeve (1/2 underarm sleeve length) from underarm fold to center fold; multiply by 2 for a total measurement.
18	SLEEVE CUFF OPENING	a. RELAXED – Measure straight across bottom of cuff/rib trim from underarm seam to center fold of sleeve, multiply by 2 for a total measurement. b. EXTENDED – Measure as above with cuff stretch fully extended.

(Continues)

HOW TO MEASURE OUTERWEAR

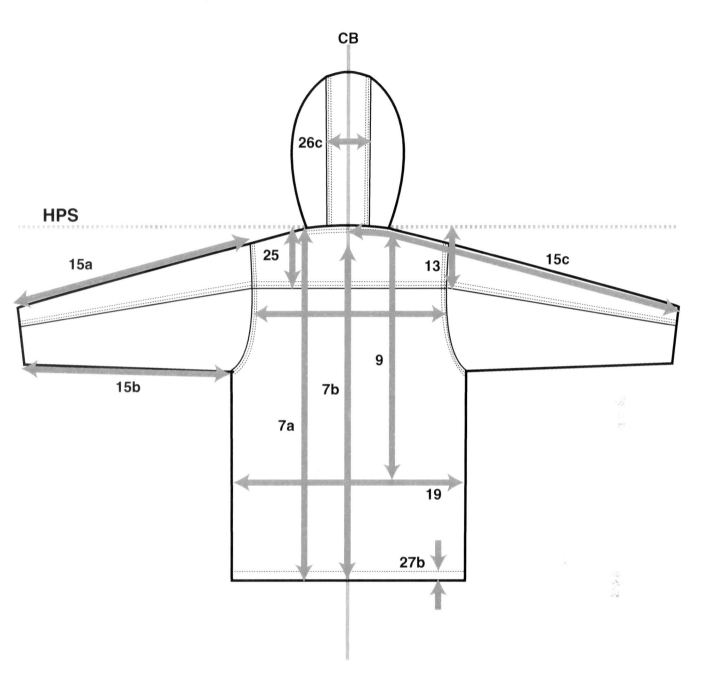

CB

HPS

26c

25

15a

13

15c

15b

9

7b

7a

19

27b

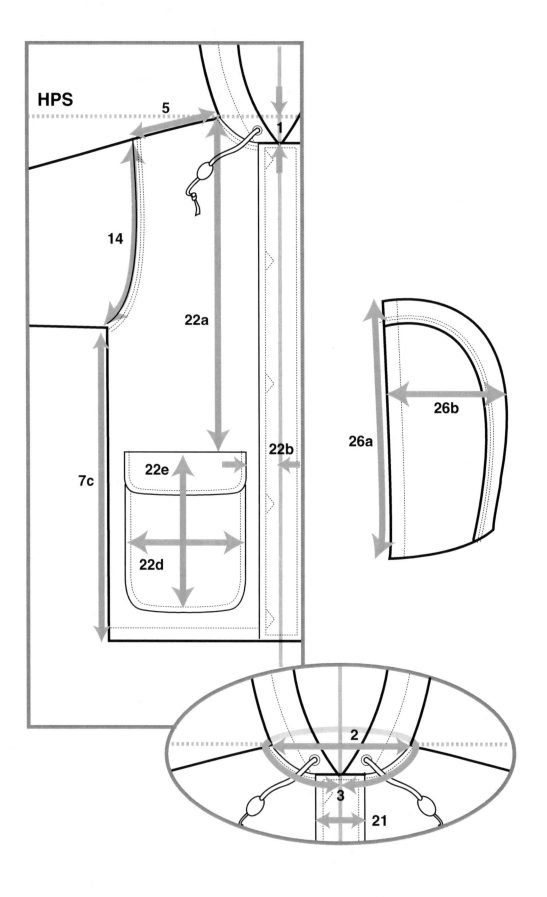

HPS

5

1

14

22a

22b

7c

22e

22d

26b

26a

2

3

21

Illustrated Measurement Points for a Hooded Jacket

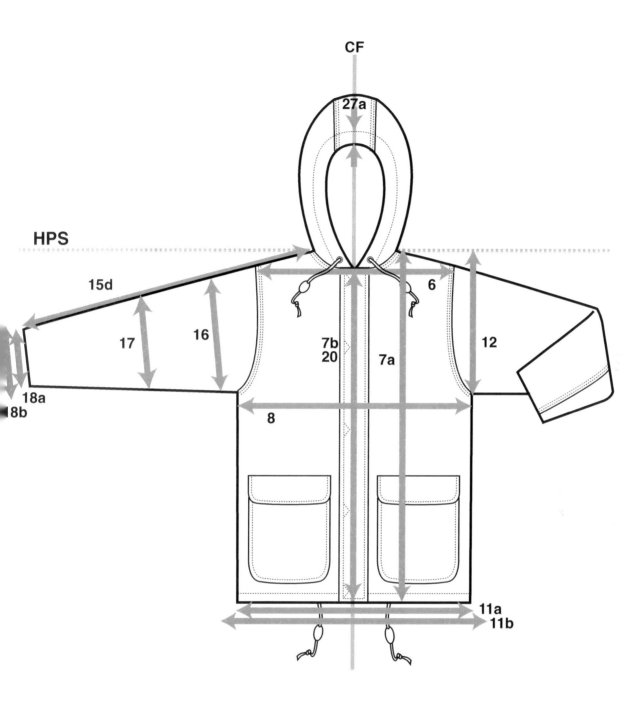

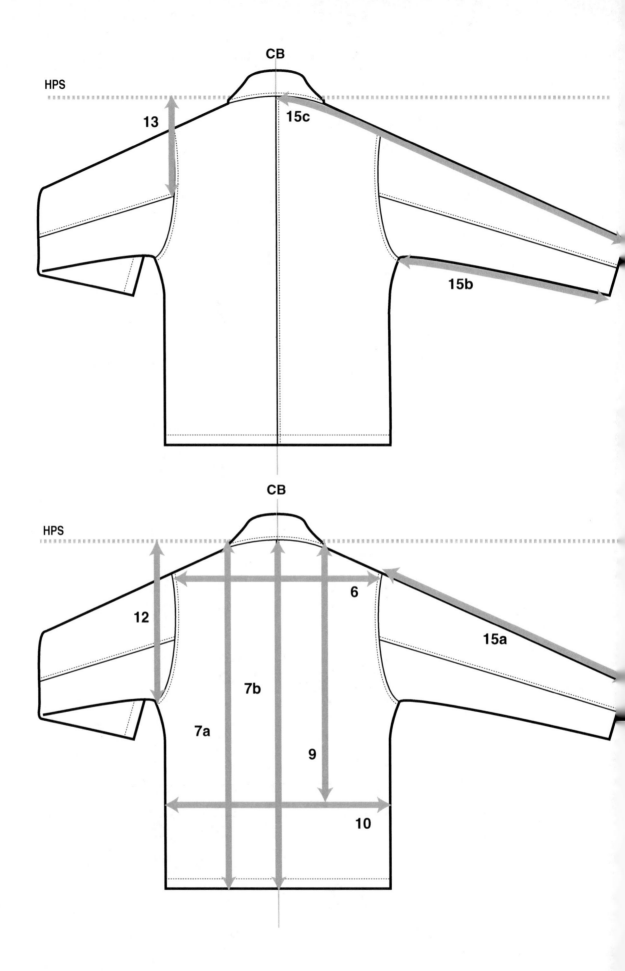

HOW TO MEASURE OUTERWEAR

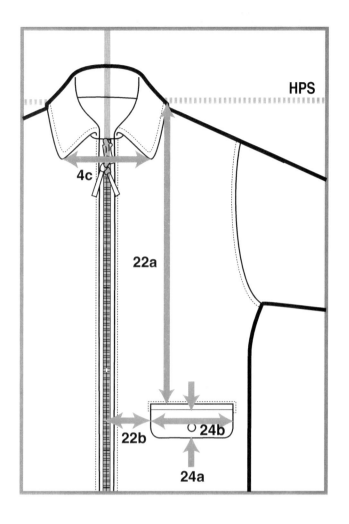

HPS

4c

22a

22b

24b

24a

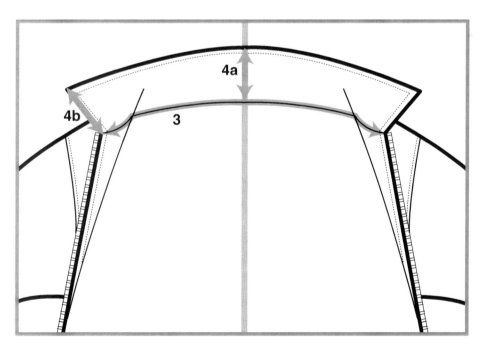

4a

4b

3

Illustrated Measurement Points for a Zipper-Entry Jacket

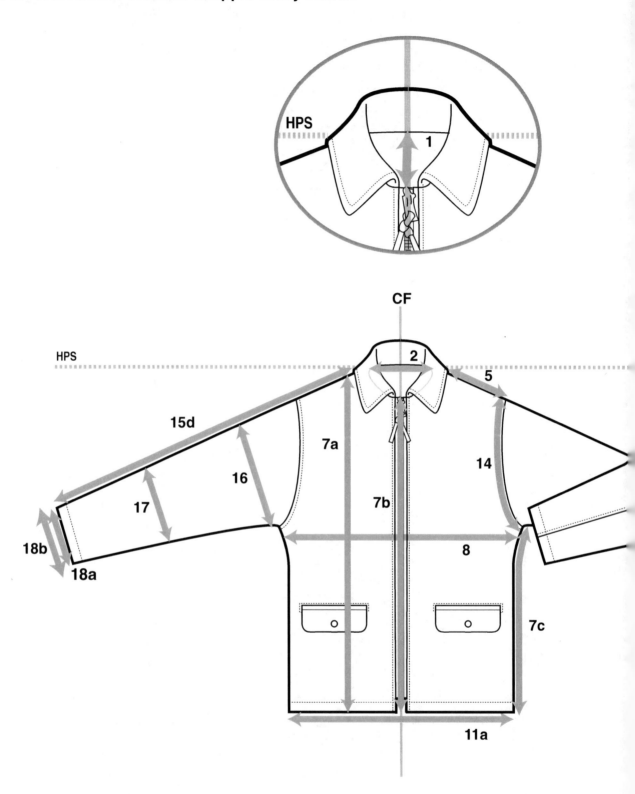

Outerwear Spec Sheet

NAME: DATE:

SEASON: STYLE: SIZE: LABEL:

DESCRIPTION:

FABRICATION/SHELL: LINING:

TRIM:

SNAPS: CORDLOCKS:

ZIPPER: DRAWSTRING:

		FRONT	BACK	TOTAL	COMMENTS
1	NECK DROP				
2	NECK – WIDTH				
3	NECK CIRCUMFERENCE				
4	COLLAR				
	a. Width @ CB				
	b. Width @ point				
	c. Spread				
5	SHOULDER – LENGTH				
6	ACROSS SHOULDER				
7	LENGTH*				
	a. HPS				
	b. CF/CB				
	c. Side				
8	ACROSS CHEST				
9	HPS TO WAIST				
10	ACROSS WAIST				
11	BOTTOM EDGE OPENING (SWEEP)				
	a. Relaxed				
	b. Extended				
12	HPS TO UNDERARM				
13	HPS TO SLEEVE SEAM				
14	ARMHOLE CIRCUMFERENCE				
15	SLEEVE – LENGTH *				
	a. Overarm				
	b. Underarm				
	c. CB				
	d. HPS				
16	UPPER SLEEVE – WIDTH @ FOLD				
17	ELBOW @ FOLD				
18	SLEEVE CUFF OPENING				
	a. Relaxed				
	b. Extended				
19	CUFF – HEIGHT				
20	FRONT PLACKET – LENGTH				
21	FRONT PLACKET – WIDTH				
22	POCKET A				
	a. Placement – HPS to top pocket edge				
	b. Placement – CF to pocket edge (top/bottom)				
	c. Placement – Side seam to pocket edge (top/bottom)				
	d. Pocket width (top/bottom)				
	e. Pocket length				
23	POCKET B				
	a. Placement – HPS to top pocket edge				
	b. Placement – CF to pocket edge (top/bottom)				
	c. Placement – Side seam to pocket edge (top/bottom)				
	d. Pocket width				
	e. Pocket length				
24	POCKET FLAP				
	a. Length				
	b. Width				
25	HPS TO YOKE				
26	HOOD				
	a. Height				
	b. Depth				
	c. Center panel				
27	DRAWCORD TUNNEL				
	a. Hood				
	b. Sweep				
28	BUTTON PLACEMENT				

REMARKS/OTHER SPECS:

* Circle method for measuring   Abbreviations: high point of shoulder (HPS), center front (CF), center back (

18 UPPER SLEEVE WIDTH	Measure straight across 1 in., or 2.54 cm, down from the armhole at a right angle to the folded edge of the sleeve.
19 ELBOW	Measure across midpoint of sleeve at a right angle to the folded edge.
20 SLEEVE OPENING	With tape measure at a right angle to the center fold of sleeve, measure straight across the bottom of sleeve.
21 SLEEVE VENT – LENGTH	Measure straight down the sleeve vent to the bottom edge of the sleeve.
22 SLEEVE PANEL FOR TWO PIECE SLEEVE	For a two piece sleeve, measure garment back from the HPS line down armhole midway to seam insertion point. Measure width of panel at underarm and at sleeve hem.
23 DEPTH OF SLEEVE HEM	Measure straight down to the fold.
24 POCKET	a. PLACEMENT – Distance from HPS – Establish the vertical placement of the pocket by measuring down from the HPS to the top of the pocket. b. PLACEMENT – Distance form CF – Establish horizontal placement of the pocket by measuring across from center front to the side of pocket. c. WIDTH – Measure across the top of the pocket. d. LENGTH – Measure down the center of the pocket. For irregularly shaped pockets, take a second measurement down the side of the pocket. e. POCKET FLAP WIDTH – Measure from top to bottom down the center of the flap. For irregularly shaped flaps, take a second measurement down the side of the flap. f. POCKET FLAP LENGTH – Measure down the center of the pocket flap. For irregularly shaped pocket flaps, take a second measurement down the side of the pocket flap.
25 POCKET B	See #24
26 POCKET C	See #24
27 BINDING – WIDTH/HEM	Measure straight down to the fold.
28 BUTTON PLACEMENT	Measure the distance of the center of the first button to the neckline seam. Measure the distance of the center of the first button to the center of the second button. Typically, buttons are evenly spaced thereafter.

1 NECK DROP	BACK – Some garments are designed with back necklines that scoop below the HPS. With the back of the garment facing you, measure at center back the distance of the back neckline from the HPS.
	FRONT – Measure down from the HPS line at center back to neckline or collar roll line at center front.
2 NECK – WIDTH	Measure straight across the neckline.
3 SHOULDER – LENGTH	Measure along the shoulder seam from the neck seam to the armhole seam.
4 ACROSS SHOULDER	Measure from shoulder point (where the shoulder seam meets the armhole seam) to shoulder point front and back.
5 ACROSS BACK	Drop 4 in., or 10.16 cm, from HPS and measure across back from armhole seam to armhole seam.
6 FRONT – LENGTH	There are several methods for measuring front length, be sure to specify which of the following you used:
	a. From HPS – Measure from the HPS straight down to the bottom of the garment. Measure both front and back.
	b. @ CF/CB – Measure down the center front of the garment from the neckline to the bottom. Measure down CB from neckline to bottom.
	c. SIDE LENGTH – Measure the side seam from the armhole to the bottom of the garment.
7 HPS TO UNDERARM	Measure from the HPS to the bottom of the armhole.
8 ACROSS CHEST	Measure garment straight across 1 in., or 2.54 cm, below armhole with garment buttoned.
9 HPS TO WAIST	Measure waist from HPS line. Women's waistlines can be located by measuring down 17 in., or 43.18 cm, from the HPS. Drop 18 in., or 45.72 cm, for men's.
10 HALF WAIST	Measure waist from CB to front edge opening on the jacket folded in half vertically. Women's waistline can be located by measuring down 17 in., or 43.18 cm, from the HPS. Drop 18 in., or 45.72 cm, for men's.
11 BOTTOM EDGE OPENING (SWEEP)	Following the contour of the hem, measure the bottom edge of the garment.
12 ARMHOLE CIRCUMFERENCE	Following the armhole seam contour, measure from the top to the bottom of the armhole. Multiply this measurement by two for the total circumference.
13 PRINCESS SEAM PLACEMENT	a. From HPS – Measure down from HPS to the point where princess seam and armhole intersect. Measure both front and back placements.
	b. From CF/CB @ armhole (or shoulder seam) – Measure across from center front to the point where princess seam intersects the armhole or shoulder seam. Also measure CB intersection point.
	c. From CF/CB @ waist – Measure across waist from center front to princess seam. Also measure CB to princess seam.
	d. From CF/CB @ sweep – Measure across bottom hem from center front to princess seam and center back to princess seam.
14 SIDE PANEL WIDTH	a. ARMHOLE – Following the armhole seam contour, measure from the shoulder to the intersection of armhole and princess seams.
	b. WAIST – Measure across side panel @ waist.
	c. SWEEP – Measure across side panel @ bottom edge opening.
15 COLLAR WIDTH	a. @ CENTER BACK – Measure at center back from the collar seam to the edge of the collar.
	b. @ POINT – Measure along the edge of the collar point to the collar seam.
16 LAPEL WIDTH @ POINT	Measure from the lapel point to the inside facing seam following a measuring direction perpendicular to center front.
17 SLEEVE – LENGTH	There are several methods for measuring sleeve length. Be sure to specify which of the following you used:
	a. OVERARM – Following the contour of the outside of the sleeve, measure from the top of the armhole seam at shoulder to bottom of the sleeve (including the cuff).
	b. UNDERARM – Measure from where the armhole and underarm seam meet to bottom of the sleeve (including the cuff).
	c. CB – With the back of the garment facing you, follow the contour of the sleeve and measure from the center back of the neckline to the bottom of the sleeve (including the cuff).
	d. HPS – Following the contour of the sleeve, measure from the HPS to the bottom of the sleeve (including the cuff).

(Continues)

How to Measure a Tailored Jacket

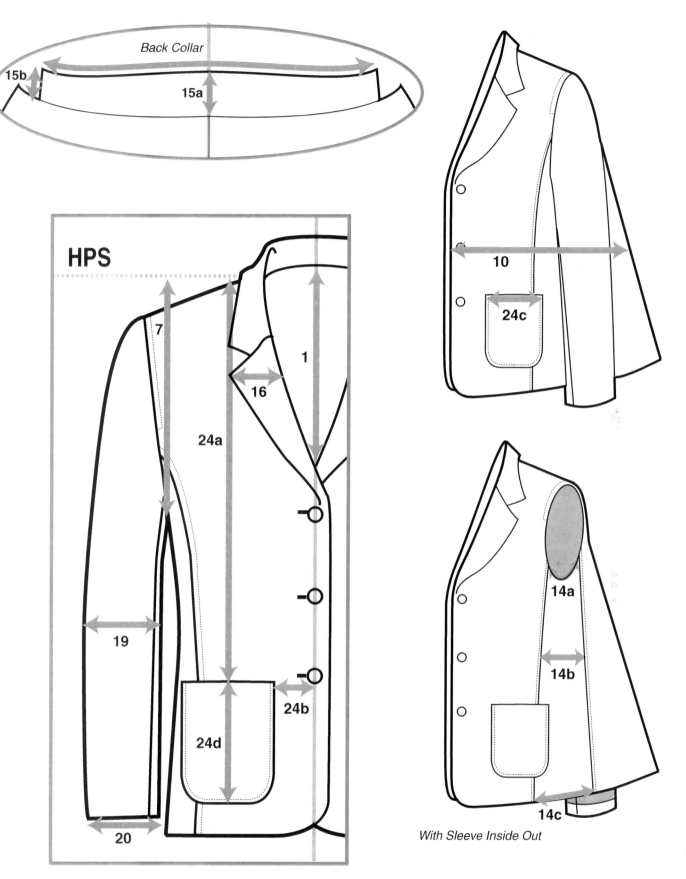

Back Collar

15b

15a

HPS

7

16

1

24a

19

20

24b

24d

10

24c

14a

14b

14c

With Sleeve Inside Out

Illustrated Measurement Points for a Tailored Jacket

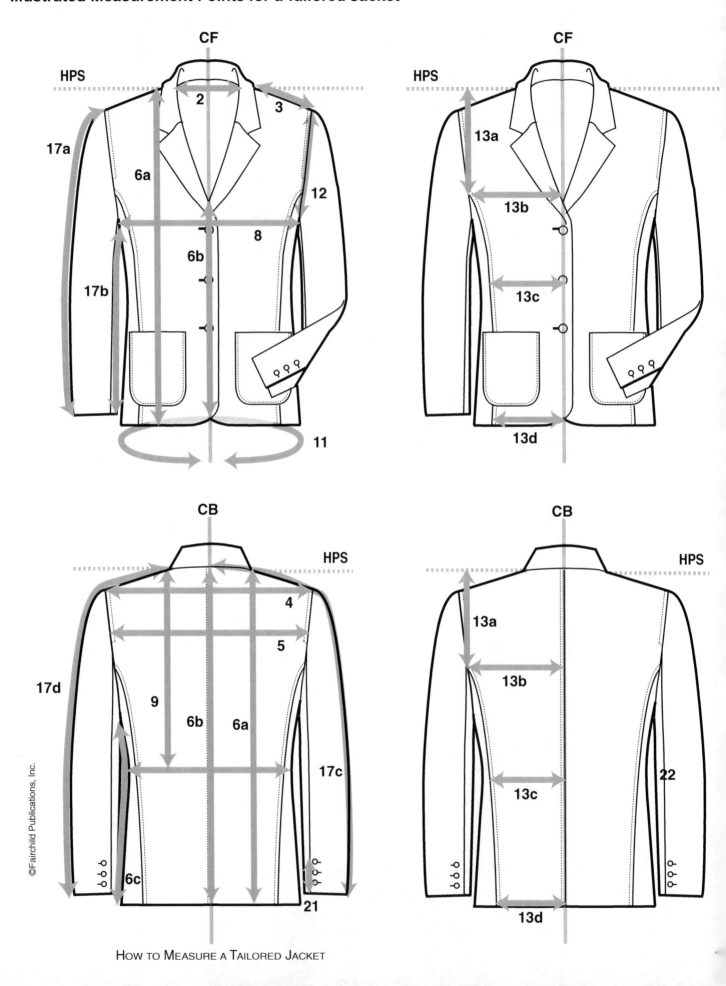

HOW TO MEASURE A TAILORED JACKET

Tailored Jacket Spec Sheet

NAME:			DATE:	
SEASON:	STYLE:	SIZE:	LABEL:	
DESCRIPTION:				

FABRICATION:

| ACCESSORIES: | | | | TRIM: | |

		FRONT	BACK	TOTAL	COMMENTS
1	NECK DROP				
2	NECK – WIDTH				
3	SHOULDER – LENGTH				
4	ACROSS SHOULDER				
5	ACROSS BACK				
6	LENGTH *				
	a. From HPS				
	b. @ CF/CB				
	c. Side				
7	HPS TO UNDERARM				
8	ACROSS CHEST				
9	HPS TO WAIST				
10	HALF WAIST				
11	BOTTOM EDGE OPENING (sweep)				
12	ARMHOLE CIRCUMFERENCE				
13	PRINCESS SEAM PLACEMENT				
	a. From HPS				
	b. From CF/CB @ armhole (or shoulder seam)				
	c. From CF/CB @ waist				
	d. From CF/CB @ sweep				
14	SIDE PANEL WIDTH				
	a. Armhole				
	b. Waist				
	c. Sweep				
15	COLLAR WIDTH				
	a. @ CENTER BACK				
	b @ POINT				
16	LAPEL WIDTH @ POINT				
17	SLEEVE – LENGTH *				
	a. Overarm				
	b. Underarm				
	c. CB				
	d. HPS				
18	UPPER SLEEVE WIDTH				
19	ELBOW				
20	SLEEVE OPENING				
21	SLEEVE VENT – LENGTH				
22	SLEEVE PANEL FOR TWO PIECE SLEEVE				
23	DEPTH OF SLEEVE HEM				
24	POCKET A				
	a. Placement – Distance from HPS				
	b. Placement – Distance From CF				
	c. Pocket width				
	d. Pocket length				
	e. Pocket flap width				
	f. Pocket flap length				
25	POCKET B				
	a. Placement – Distance from HPS				
	b. Placement – Distance From CF				
	c. Pocket width				
	d. Pocket length				
	e. Pocket flap width				
	f. Pocket flap length				
26	POCKET C				
	a. Placement – Distance from HPS				
	b. Placement – Distance From CF				
	c. Pocket width				
	d. Pocket length				
	e. Pocket flap width				
	f. Pocket flap length				
27	BINDING – WIDTH/HEM				
28	BUTTON PLACEMENT				

REMARKS/OTHER SPECS:

* Circle method for measuring   Abbreviations: high point of shoulder (HPS), center front (CF), center back (

HOW TO MEASURE A TAILORED JACKET

19	SLEEVE – LENGTH/ RAGLAN	There are several methods for measuring sleeve length. Be sure to specify which of the following you use: a. OVERARM – Following the contour of the outside of the sleeve, measure from the top of the neckline seam to the bottom of the sleeve (including the cuff). b. UNDERARM – Measure from where the armhole and underarm seam meet to bottom of the sleeve (including the cuff). c. CB – With the back of the garment facing you, follow the contour of the sleeve and measure from the center back of the neckline to the bottom of the sleeve (including the cuff).
20	UPPER SLEEVE – WIDTH	Measure straight across 1 in., or 2.54 cm, down from the armhole at a right angle to the folded edge of the sleeve.
21	ELBOW	Measure across midpoint of sleeve at a right angle to the folded edge.
22	CUFF WIDTH AT TRANSFER POINT	Measure at transfer point (where sleeve knit stitch changes to the rib stitch) horizontally from side to side.
23	CUFF OPENING	a. RELAXED – Measure straight across bottom of cuff/rib trim from underarm seam to center fold of sleeve, both front and back. b. EXTENDED – Measure as above with cuff stretch fully extended.
24	CUFF TRIM – HEIGHT	Measure straight down from top of transfer point to bottom of cuff.
25	BODY TRIM – HEIGHT	Measure trim vertically from transfer point to bottom of trim.
26	FRONT PLACKET	a. LENGTH – Measure length of front placket vertically down center front from neckline seam to bottom. b. WIDTH – Measure across the placket.
27	POCKET A	a. PLACEMENT – Distance from HPS – establish the vertical placement of the pocket by measuring down from the HPS line to the top edge of the pocket. b. PLACEMENT – Distance from CF – establish the horizontal placement of the pocket by measuring across from the center front to the side edge of the pocket. c. WIDTH – Measure across the top of the pocket. d. LENGTH – Measure down the center of the pocket. For irregularly shaped pockets, take a second measurement down the side of the pocket.
28	POCKET B	a. PLACEMENT – distance from HPS – establish the vertical placement of the pocket by measuring down from the HPS line to the top edge of the pocket. b. PLACEMENT – distance from CF – establish the horizontal placement of the pocket by measuring across from the center front to the side edge of the pocket. c. WIDTH – Measure across the top of the pocket. d. LENGTH – Measure down the center of the pocket. For irregularly shaped pockets, take a second measurement down the side of the pocket.
29	BUTTON PLACEMENT	Measure the distance of the center of the first button to the neckline seam. Measure the distance of the center of the first button to the center of the second button. Typically, buttons are evenly spaced thereafter.

1 NECK DROP	BACK – Some knits are designed with back necklines that scoop below the HPS line. With the back of the garment facing you, measure at center back the distance of the back neckline from the HPS line.
	FRONT – Measure down center front from HPS line to the neckline seam.
2 NECK – WIDTH	Measure neck straight across at the neckline.
3 NECK CIRCUMFERENCE	a. RELAXED – Measure front neckline beginning at the shoulder seam following neck edge to opposite shoulder seam. Continue measuring the back neckline.
	b. EXTENDED – Measure as above with neck stretch fully extended.
4 COLLAR – HEIGHT	a. CENTER FRONT – Unroll collar if folded and measure from center front collar seam to top edge of collar.
	b. CENTER BACK – Unroll collar if folded and measure from center back collar seam to top edge of collar.
5 NECK OPENING AT TOP OF TRIM	a. RELAXED – Measure horizontally across top of neck trim/collar from one side to the other.
	b. EXTENDED – Measure as above with neck trim stretch fully extended.
6 SHOULDER – LENGTH	For set-in sleeves, measure along the shoulder seam from the neck seam to the armhole seam.
7 ACROSS SHOULDER	For set-in sleeves, measure from shoulder point (where the shoulder seam meets the armhole seam) to shoulder point both front and back.
8 SHOULDER SLOPE FROM HPS	Measure vertically from the HPS line to the top edge of the armhole seam.
9 LENGTH	There are several methods for measuring front length. Be sure to specify which of the following you use:
	a. HPS – Measure down front/back of sweater from HPS line to bottom of knit.
	b. CF/CB – Measure down center front/center back from neckline to bottom of knit.
	c. SIDE – Measure the side seam from the armhole to the bottom of the garment.
10 HPS TO UNDERARM	Measure vertically down from the HPS line to bottom edge of underarm.
11 ARMHOLE CIRCUMFERENCE	Following the armhole seam contour, measure from the shoulder point to the bottom of the armhole. Use this method for measuring set-in sleeves.
12 RAGLAN SEAM	Measure front and back raglan seams from neckline seam to underarm seam.
13 ACROSS CHEST	Measure garment straight across 1 in., or 2.54 cm, below armhole.
14 WAIST MEASUREMENT FROM HPS	Measure down 17 in., or 43.18 cm, from the HPS line to locate a woman's waistline. Drop 18 in., or 45.72 cm, for a man's waist.
15 ACROSS WAIST	Locate waist from HPS line. Then, measure horizontally across waist from side to side.
16 BOTTOM EDGE OPENING (SWEEP)	a. RELAXED – Measure bottom edge following the contour of the knit.
	b. EXTENDED – Measure as above with stretch fully extended.
17 BODY WIDTH AT TRANSFER POINT	Measure transfer point (where body knit stitch changes to the rib stitch) horizontally from side to side.
18 SLEEVE – LENGTH/SET-IN	There are several methods for measuring sleeve length. Be sure to specify which of the following you use:
	a. OVERARM – Following the contour of the outside of the sleeve, measure from top of armhole seam at the shoulder to the bottom of the sleeve (including the cuff).
	b. UNDERARM – Measure from where the armhole and underarm seam meet to bottom of the sleeve (including the cuff).
	c. CB – With the back of the garment facing you, following the contour of the sleeve, measure from the center back of the neckline to the bottom of the sleeve (including the cuff).
	d. HPS – Following the contour of the sleeve, measure from the HPS to the bottom of the sleeve (including the cuff).

(Continues)

HOW TO MEASURE A SWEATER

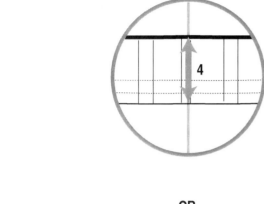

4

CB

HPS

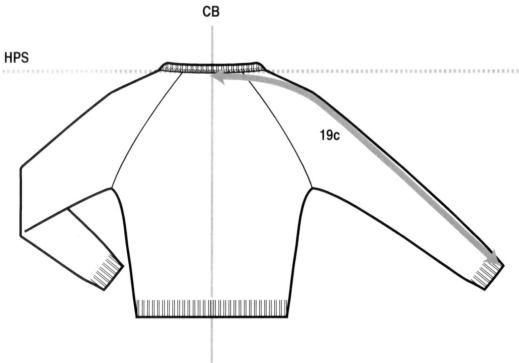

19c

Illustrated Measurement Points for a Cardigan with Raglan Armhole

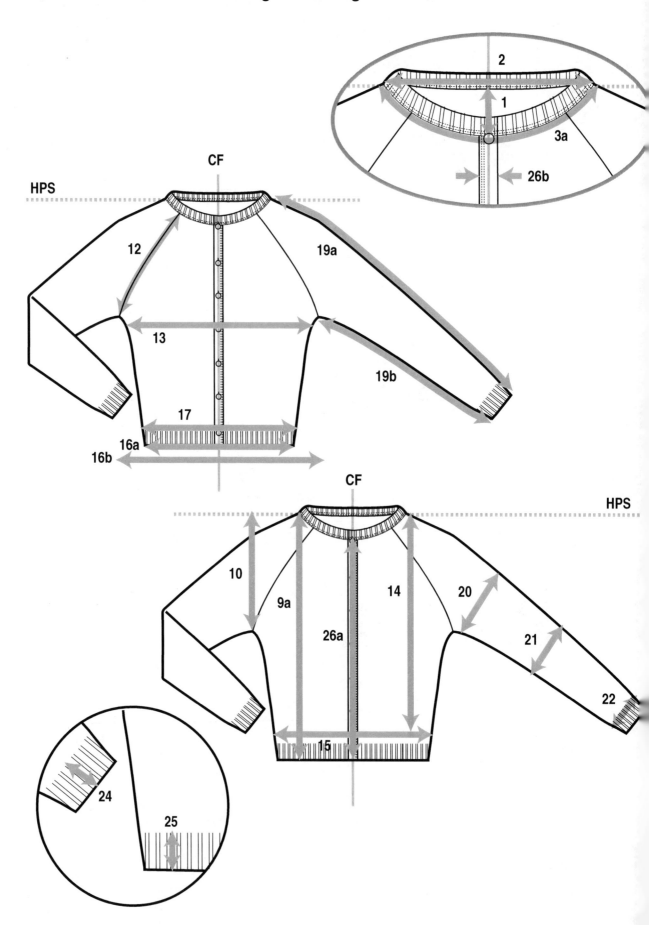

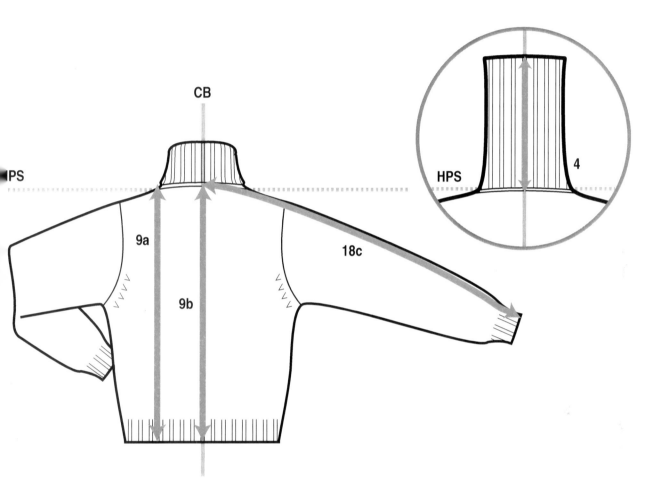

CB

IPS

9a

9b

18c

HPS

4

Illustrated Measurement Points for a Pullover

Sweater Spec Sheet

NAME:			DATE:	
SEASON:	STYLE:	SIZE:		LABEL:
DESCRIPTION:				

FABRICATION:

ACCESSORIES:		TRIM:

KNIT STITCHES:

	FRONT	BACK	TOTAL	COMMENTS
1 NECK DROP				
2 NECK – WIDTH				
3 NECK CIRCUMFERENCE				
a. Relaxed				
b. Extended				
4 COLLAR HEIGHT @ CF/CB				
5 NECK OPENING AT TOP OF TRIM				
a. Relaxed				
b. Extended				
6 SHOULDER – LENGTH				
7 ACROSS SHOULDER				
8 SHOULDER SLOPE FROM HPS				
9 LENGTH *				
a. HPS				
b. CF/CB				
c. Side				
10 HPS TO UNDERARM				
11 ARMHOLE CIRCUMFERENCE				
12 RAGLAN SEAM				
13 ACROSS CHEST				
14 WAIST MEASURE FROM HPS				
15 ACROSS WAIST				
16 SWEEP				
a. Relaxed				
b. Extended				
17 BODY WIDTH AT TRANSFER POINT				
18 SLEEVE - LENGTH / Set-In *				
a. Overarm				
b. Underarm				
c. CB				
d. HPS				
19 SLEEVE - LENGTH / Raglan *				
a. Overarm				
b. Underarm				
c. CB				
20 UPPER SLEEVE – WIDTH				
21 ELBOW				
22 CUFF WIDTH AT TRANSFER POINT				
23 CUFF OPENING				
a. Relaxed				
b. Extended				
24 CUFF TRIM – HEIGHT				
25 BODY TRIM – HEIGHT				
26 FRONT PLACKET				
a. Length				
b. Width				
27 POCKET A				
a. Placement - distance from HPS				
b. Placement - distance from CF				
c. Pocket Width				
d. Pocket Length				
28 POCKET B				
a. Placement - distance from HPS				
b. Placement - distance from CF				
c. Pocket Width				
d. Pocket Length				
29 BUTTON PLACEMENT				

REMARKS/OTHER SPECS:

* Circle method for measuring   Abbreviations: high point of shoulder (HPS), center front (CF), center back

HOW TO MEASURE A SWEATER

21 CUFF/SLEEVE BOTTOM	a. RELAXED – Measure straight across bottom of sleeve /cuff from underarm seam to center fold of sleeve.
	b. EXTENDED – Measure as above with garment stretch fully extended.
22 LENGTH TO LEG BOTTOM	a. RELAXED – Measure from center back of neck to center of bottom pant opening.
	b. EXTENDED – Measure as above with garment stretch fully extended.
23 INSEAM	Measure from crotch (where rise seam and inseam intersect) following inseam down to bottom of pant opening.
24 THIGH CIRCUMFERENCE	Measure thigh inseam down 1 in., or 2.54 cm, below crotch. At this point, measure across leg from inseam to side seam both front and back.
25 KNEE CIRCUMFERENCE	For womenswear, determine the knee position* by measuring inseam down 12″ below crotch. At this point, measure across leg from inseam to side seam both front and back.
	* Knee positions for other categories: Petites: 11 in., or 27.94 cm, Plus Size: 13 in., or 33.02 cm, Junior: 12 in., or 30.48 cm, Boys and Girls: 1.5 in., or 3.81 cm, less than half the finished inseam length; Mens: 2 in., or 5.08 cm, less than half the finished inseam length.
26 BOTTOM OPENING	Measure the bottom edge of the pant leg from inseam to side seam both front and back.
27 COLLAR	a. WIDTH CB – Measure at center back from the collar seam to the edge of the collar.
	b. WIDTH @ POINT – Measure along the edge of the collar point.
	c. SPREAD – Measure across between the points of the collar.
28 PLACKET	a. WIDTH – Measure straight across the front closure placket from edge to edge.
	b. LENGTH – Measure straight down center front from top to bottom of placket.
29 POCKET	a. PLACEMENT – Distance from HPS – Measure down from HPS line to the top of the pocket.
	b. PLACEMENT – Distance from CF – Measure across from CF to side of pocket.
	c. POCKET WIDTH – Measure across top edge of pocket.
	d. POCKET LENGTH – Measure vertically down center of pocket from top to bottom.
	e. POCKET FLAP – WIDTH – Measure horizontally across pocket flap from edge to edge.
	f. POCKET FLAP – LENGTH – Measure from top to bottom down center of flap.
30 BUTTON PLACEMENT	Measure the distance of the center of the first button to the neckline seam. Measure the distance of the center of the first button to the center of the second button. Typically, buttons are evenly spaced thereafter.

1	NECK DROP	BACK – Some garments are designed with back necklines that scoop below the HPS line. With the back of the garment facing you, measure at center back the distance of the back neckline from the HPS line.
		FRONT – Measure down center front from HPS line to the neckline seam.
2	NECK – WIDTH	Measure straight across the neckline.
3	NECK CIRCUMFERENCE	Measure front and back neckline beginning at shoulder seam following neck edge to opposite shoulder seam.
4	SHOULDER – LENGTH	Measure along the shoulder seam from the neck seam to the armhole seam.
5	ACROSS SHOULDER	Measure from shoulder point (where the shoulder seam meets the armhole seam) to shoulder point.
6	TORSO – LENGTH	There are several methods for measuring front length. Be sure to specify which of the following you use: a. HPS to crotch relaxed – Measure front from shoulder seam at HPS to crotch. b. HPS to crotch extended – For extended measurements, stretch garment until fully extended and measure as for #6a. c. CF/CB length relaxed – Measure down center front/center back of garment from neckline to crotch. d. CF/CB length extended – For extended measurements, stretch garment until fully extended and measure as for #6c.
7	ACROSS BACK	Measure down 4 in., or 10.16 cm, from HPS line. At this point, measure across back from one armhole seam to the other.
8	HPS TO UNDERARM	Measure perpendicularly from the HPS line to the bottom of the underarm.
9	ACROSS CHEST	Measure garment straight across 1 in., or 2.54 cm, below armhole, both front and back.
10	HPS TO WAIST	Measure down center back from HPS line to the waistline; the women's waistline is approximately 17 in., or 43.18 cm, from the HPS.
11	ACROSS WAIST	a. RELAXED – Measure from side to side. b. EXTENDED – Measure as above with garment stretch fully extended.
12	HIGH HIP	Locate the high hip position by dropping 4 in., or 10.16 cm, from natural waist. Measure from side seam to side seam, both front and back.
13	LOW HIP	Locate the low hip position* by dropping 7 in., or 17.78 cm, from natural waist. Measure from side seam to side seam, both front and back. * Low hip positions for other categories: Juniors, Petites, Plus: Measure as above; Girls and Boys: Measure up 2.5 in., or 6.35 cm, from crotch; Mens: measure up 3 in., or 7.62 cm, from crotch
14	LEG OPENING	a. RELAXED – Measure along leg opening contour from side seam to crotch both front and back. b. EXTENDED – Measure as above with the garment stretch fully extended.
15	CROTCH – WIDTH	Measure horizontally across fold of crotch.
16	RISE	FRONT – Measuring from the crotch (the point where the rise seam intersects the inseam), follow the contour of the front rise seam to the waistline. BACK – Measuring from the crotch (the point where the rise seam intersects the inseam), follow the contour of the back rise seam to the waistline.
17	ARMHOLE CIRCUMFERENCE	Following the armhole seam contour, measure from the shoulder point to the bottom of the armhole. The sum of front and back measurements equal the total circumference.
18	UPPER SLEEVE – WIDTH	Measure straight across 1 in., or 2.54 cm, down from the armhole at a right angle to the folded edge of the sleeve both front and back.
19	ELBOW	Measure across midpoint of sleeve at a right angle to the folded edge both front and back.
20	SLEEVE – LENGTH	There are several methods for measuring sleeve length. Be sure to specify which of the following you use: a. Following the contour of the outside of the sleeve, measure from top of the armhole seam at shoulder to the bottom of the sleeve (including the cuff). b. Measure from where the armhole and underarm seam meet to bottom of the sleeve (including the cuff). c. With the back of the garment facing you, follow the contour of the sleeve and measure from the center back of the neckline to the bottom of the sleeve (including the cuff). d. Following the contour of the sleeve, measure from the HPS to the bottom of the sleeve (including the cuff).

(Continues)

HOW TO MEASURE BODYSUITS AND JUMPSUITS

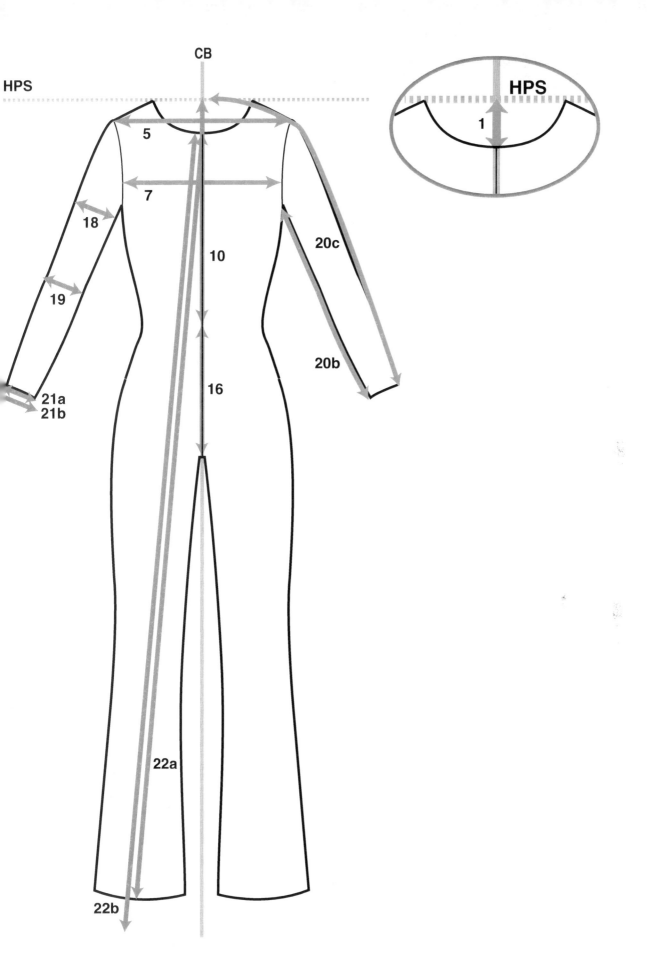

HPS

CB

5

7

18

19

21a
21b

10

16

20c

20b

22a

22b

HPS

HPS

1

Illustrated Measurement Points for a Jumpsuit

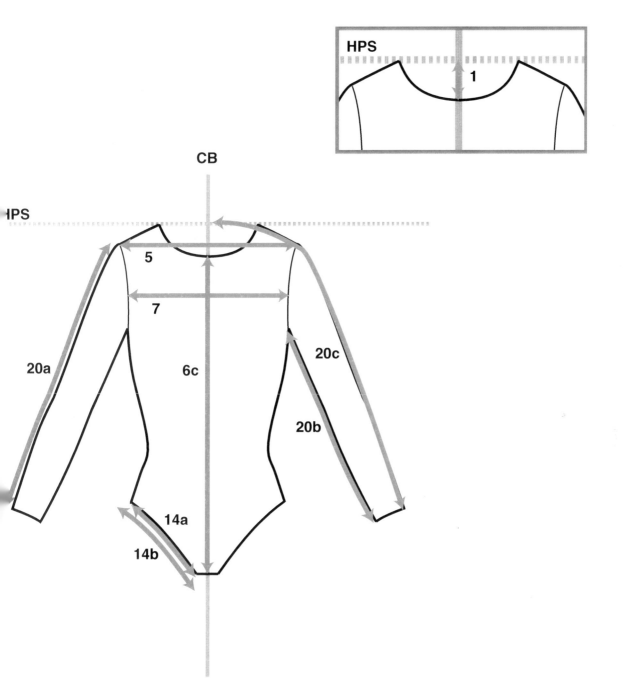

HPS

1

CB

HPS

5

7

20a

6c

20c

20b

14a

14b

Illustrated Measurement Points for a Bodysuit

HOW TO MEASURE BODYSUITS AND JUMPSUITS

Bodysuits and Jumpsuits Spec Sheet

NAME:			DATE:		
SEASON:		STYLE:	SIZE:	LABEL:	
DESCRIPTION:					

FABRICATION:

ACCESSORIES: TRIM:

		FRONT	BACK	TOTAL	COMMENTS
1	NECK DROP				
2	NECK – WIDTH				
3	NECK CIRCUMFERENCE				
4	SHOULDER – LENGTH				
5	ACROSS SHOULDER				
6	TORSO – LENGTH *				
	a. HPS to crotch relaxed				
	b. HPS to crotch extended				
	c. CF/CB length relaxed				
	d. CF/CB length extended				
7	ACROSS BACK				
8	HPS TO UNDERARM				
9	ACROSS CHEST				
10	HPS TO WAIST				
11	ACROSS WAIST				
	a. Relaxed				
	b. Extended				
12	HIGH HIP (4 in., or 10.16 cm, from natural waist)				
13	LOW HIP (7 in., or 17.78 cm, from natural waist)				
14	LEG OPENING				
	a. relaxed				
	b. extended				
15	CROTCH – WIDTH				
16	RISE				
17	ARMHOLE CIRCUMFERENCE				
18	UPPER SLEEVE – WIDTH				
19	ELBOW				
20	SLEEVE – LENGTH *				
	a. Overarm				
	b. Underarm				
	c. CB				
	d. HPS				
21	CUFF/SLEEVE BOTTOM				
	a. Relaxed				
	b. Extended				
22	CB LENGTH TO LEG BOTTOM				
	a. Relaxed				
	b. Extended				
23	INSEAM				
24	THIGH CIRCUMFERENCE				
25	KNEE CIRCUMFERENCE				
26	BOTTOM OPENING				
27	COLLAR				
	a. Width - CB				
	b. Width @ point				
	c. Spread				
28	PLACKET				
	a. Width				
	b. Length				
29	POCKET				
	a. Placement – Distance from HPS				
	b. Placement – Distance From CF				
	c. Pocket width				
	d. Pocket length				
	e. Pocket flap width				
	f. Pocket flap length				
30	BUTTON PLACEMENT				

REMARKS/OTHER SPECS:

* Circle method for measuring   Abbreviations: high point of shoulder (HPS), center front (CF), center back

HOW TO MEASURE BODYSUITS AND JUMPSUITS

18	ELBOW	Measure across midpoint of sleeve at a right angle to the folded edge front and back.
19	SLEEVE HEM/CUFF OPENING	a. RELAXED – Measure straight across the bottom edge of the cuff.
		b. EXTENDED – Measure as above with garment stretch fully extended.
20	DEPTH OF SLEEVE HEM	Measure straight down to the fold.
21	CUFF – HEIGHT	Measure straight down from top to bottom of cuff.
22	DART PLACEMENT	a. PLACEMENT – CF/CB to top of dart – Measure across from center front center back to the top of the dart.
		b. PLACEMENT – HPS to top of dart – Measure down from HPS line to top of the dart.
		c. PLACEMENT – CF/CB to bottom of dart – Measure across from center front center back to the bottom of the dart.
		d. PLACEMENT – HPS to bottom of dart – Measure down from HPS line to bottom of the dart.
		e. DART – LENGTH – Measure dart length from top to bottom.
23	BINDING – WIDTH/HEM	Measure top edge hem straight down to the fold.
24	BUTTON PLACEMENT	Measure the distance of the first button to the neckline seam. Measure the distance of the center of the first button to the center of the second button. Typically, buttons are evenly spaced thereafter.

1	NECK DROP	BACK – Some garments are designed with back necklines that drop below the HPS. With the back of the garment facing you, measure at center back the distance of the back neckline from the HPS line.
		FRONT – Measure down from the HPS line at center back to the neckline or collar seam.
2	NECK – WIDTH	Measure straight across the neckline.
3	NECK CIRCUMFERENCE	Measure neckline following the contour of the neck seam, both front and back.
4	SHOULDER – LENGTH	Measure along the shoulder seam from the neck seam to the armhole seam.
5	ACROSS SHOULDER	Measure from shoulder point (where the shoulder seam meets the armhole seam) to shoulder point.
6	LENGTH	There are several methods for measuring front length. Be sure to specify which of the following you use:
		a. HPS – Measure from the HPS straight down to the bottom of the garment. Measure both front and back length of garment.
		b. CF/CB – Measure down the center front of the garment from the neckline to the bottom edge. Also measure down center back of garment.
		c. SIDE – Measure the side seam from the armhole to the bottom of the garment. If the garment has slit, measure to where the slit begins.
7	ACROSS BACK	Measure down 4 in., or 10.16 cm, from the HPS line at center back. Then measure across from one armhole seam to the other.
8	ACROSS CHEST	Measure garment straight across 1 in., or 2.54 cm, below armhole.
9	WAIST – LENGTH	There are several methods for measuring front waist length. Be sure to specify which of the following you use:
		a. CF/CB – With the front of the garment facing you, measure down the center front from the neckline seam to the waist. Measure down center back from neckline seam to waist.
		b. HPS – Measure from the HPS straight down to waist, both front and back.
10	ACROSS WAIST	a. RELAXED – Determine (#9) front and back waist length; measure from side to side, both front and back.
		b. EXTENDED – Measure as above with stretch fully extended.
11	HIGH HIP	Measure 4 in., or 10.16 cm, down from garment waist. Then measure high hip from side seam to side seam, front and back.
12	LOW HIP	Measure 7 in., or 17.78 cm, down from garment waist. Then measure low hip from side seam to side seam, front and back.
13	BOTTOM EDGE OPENING (SWEEP)	Make sure that any pleats or gathers are fully extended. Then, following the contour of the hem, measure the bottom edge of the garment front and back.
14	HPS TO UNDERARM	Measure perpendicularly from the HPS line to the bottom of the armhole.
15	ARMHOLE CIRCUMFERENCE	Following the armhole seam contour, measure from the shoulder point to the bottom of the armhole. Measure both front and back of armhole.
16	UPPER SLEEVE – WIDTH	Measure straight across 1 in., or 2.54 cm, down from the armhole at a right angle to the folded edge of the sleeve.
17	SLEEVE – LENGTH	There are several methods for measuring sleeve length. Be sure to specify which of the following you use:
		a. OVERARM – Following the contour of the outside of the sleeve, measure from the top of the armhole seam at shoulder to the bottom of the sleeve (including the cuff).
		b. UNDERARM – Measure from where the armhole and underarm seam meet to bottom of the sleeve (including the cuff).
		c. CB – With the back of the garment facing you, follow the contour of the sleeve and measure from the center back of the neckline to the bottom of the sleeve (including the cuff).
		d. HPS – Following the contour of the sleeve, measure from the HPS to the bottom of the sleeve (including the cuff).

(Continues)

HOW TO MEASURE A DRESS

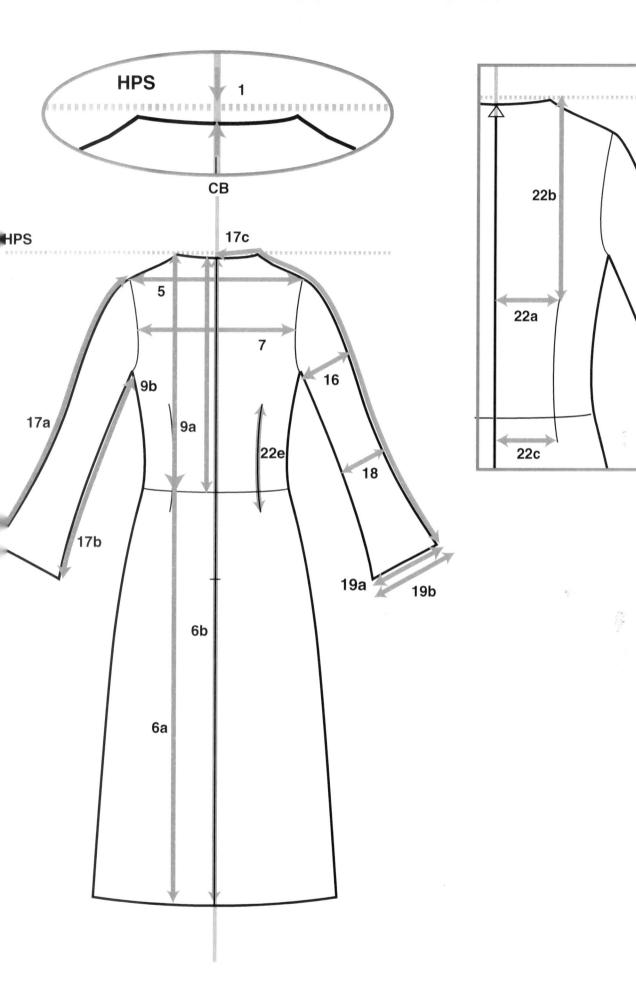

HPS

1

CB

HPS

17c

5

7

16

9b

17a

9a

22e

18

17b

6b

19a

19b

6a

22b

22a

22c

Illustrated Measurement Points for a Dress

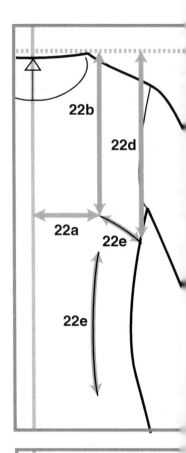

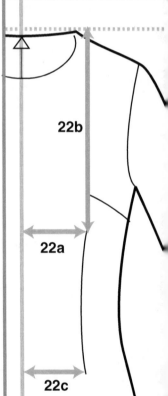

2

1

3

CF

HPS

9b

4

9a

14

15

8

17d

10a
10b

11

12

6a

6b

6c

13

22b

22d

22a

22e

22e

22b

22a

22c

Dress Spec Sheet

NAME:		DATE:		
SEASON:	STYLE:	SIZE:	LABEL:	
DESCRIPTION:				

FABRICATION:

ACCESSORIES: | TRIM:

		FRONT	BACK	TOTAL	COMMENTS
1	NECK DROP				
2	NECK – WIDTH				
3	NECK CIRCUMFERENCE				
4	SHOULDER – LENGTH				
5	ACROSS SHOULDER				
6	LENGTH *				
	a. HPS				
	b. CF/CB				
	c. Side				
7	ACROSS BACK				
8	ACROSS CHEST				
9	WAIST – LENGTH *				
	a. CF/CB				
	b. HPS				
10	ACROSS WAIST				
	a. Relaxed				
	b. Extended				
11	HIGH HIP (4 in., or 10.16 cm, from natural waist)				
12	LOW HIP (7 in., or 17.78 cm, from natural waist)				
13	BOTTOM EDGE OPENING (SWEEP)				
14	HPS TO UNDERARM				
15	ARMHOLE CIRCUMFERENCE				
16	UPPER SLEEVE – WIDTH				
17	SLEEVE – LENGTH *				
	a. Overarm				
	b. Underarm				
	c. CB				
	d. HPS				
18	ELBOW				
19	SLEEVE HEM/CUFF OPENING				
	a. Relaxed				
	b. Extended				
20	DEPTH OF SLEEVE HEM				
21	CUFF HEIGHT				
22	DART				
	a. Placement – CF/CB to top of dart				
	b. Placement – HPS to top of dart				
	c. Placement – CF/CB to bottom of dart				
	d. Placement – HPS to bottom of dart				
	e. Dart – Length				
23	BINDING WIDTH/HEM				
24	BUTTON PLACEMENT				

REMARKS/OTHER SPECS/STITCHING:

* Circle method for measuring   Abbreviations: high point of shoulder (HPS), center front (CF), center back (

HOW TO MEASURE A DRESS

20	DEPTH OF SLEEVE HEM	Measure straight down to the fold.
21	BINDING – WIDTH/HEM	Measure straight down to the fold.
22	FRONT PLACKET – WIDTH	Measure across the placket.
23	YOKE	Measure down from HPS line.
24	POCKET	a. PLACEMENT – distance from HPS – Establish the vertical placement of the pocket by measuring down from the HPS line to the top of the pocket. b. PLACEMENT – distance from CF – Establish horizontal placement of pocket by measuring across from the center front to the side of pocket. c. POCKET WIDTH – Measure horizontally across top of pocket from edge to edge. d. POCKET LENGTH – Measure vertically down center of pocket from the top to the bottom. For irregularly shaped pockets, also measure down side of pocket. e. POCKET FLAP WIDTH – Measure horizontally across pocket flap from edge to edge. f. POCKET FLAP LENGTH – Measure from top to bottom down center of flap. For irregular shaping, measure down side of flap.
25	PLEATS	a. PLACEMENT – distance from CF/CB – Measure the distance of the pleat to the center front/center back. b. DEPTH – Measure depth of pleats
26	DART	a. PLACEMENT from HPS – Measure down vertically from HPS to top of dart. b. PLACEMENT from CF/CB – Measure horizontally from CF/CB to dart seam. c. LENGTH – Measure dart length from top to bottom.
27	BUTTON PLACEMENT	Measure the distance of the center of the first button to the neckline seam. Measure the distance of the center of the first button to the center of the second button. Typically, buttons are evenly spaced thereafter.

Table of Measurement Points for a Woven Shirt

1 NECK DROP	BACK – Some garments are designed with back necklines that scoop below the HPS; with the back of the garment facing you, measure at center back the distance of the back neckline from the HPS line.
	FRONT – Measure down from the HPS line at center back to the neckline or collar seam at center front.
2 NECK – WIDTH	Measure straight across the neckline.
3 SHOULDER – LENGTH	Measure along the shoulder seam from the neck seam to the armhole seam.
4 ACROSS SHOULDER	Measure horizontally from shoulder point (where the shoulder seam meets the armhole seam) to shoulder point, both front and back.
5 LENGTH	There are several methods for measuring front length. Be sure to specify which of the following you use: a. HPS – Measure CF from the HPS straight down to the bottom of the garment. Also measure CB from HPS to bottom. b. CF/CB – Measure down the center front of the garment from the neckline to the bottom. Measure down center back from neckline to bottom. c. SIDE – Measure side seam from armhole vertically to bottom of garment. For slits, measure to where slit begins.
6 HPS TO UNDERARM	Measure perpendicularly from the HPS line to the bottom of the armhole.
7 ACROSS CHEST	Measure garment straight across 1 in., or 2.54 cm, below armhole, both front and back.
8 ACROSS WAIST	Measure from side to side at narrowest point, both front and back. The womenswear waistline can be located by measuring down 17 in., or 43.18 cm, from the HPS. Drop 18 in., or 45.72 cm, for men.
9 BOTTOM EDGE OPENING (SWEEP)	Make sure that any pleats or gathers are fully extended and following the contour of the hem. Then measure bottom edge of the garment.
10 COLLAR BAND	a. HEIGHT – Measure at center back from neckline seam to top edge of collar band. b. LENGTH – Measure along the center of the collar band from center of button to the end of the buttonhole.
11 COLLAR	a. WIDTH @ CENTER BACK – Measure at center back from the collar seam to the top edge of the collar. b. WIDTH @ POINT – Measure along the edge of the collar point. c. SPREAD – Measure across between the points of the collar.
12 ARMHOLE CIRCUMFERENCE	Following the armhole seam contour, measure from top of the shoulder seam to bottom of armhole. The sum of the front and back measurements equal the total circumference.
13 UPPER SLEEVE WIDTH	Measure straight across 1 in., or 2.54 cm, down from the armhole at a right angle to the folded edge of the sleeve.
14 SLEEVE LENGTH	There are several methods for measuring sleeve length. Be sure to specify which of the following you use: a. OVERARM – Following the contour of the outside of the sleeve, measure from top of armhole seam at the shoulder to the bottom of the sleeve (including the cuff). b. UNDERARM – Measure from where the armhole and underarm seams meet to bottom of the sleeve (including the cuff). c. CB – With the back of the garment facing you, follow the contour of the sleeve and measure from the center back of the neckline to the bottom of the sleeve (including the cuff). d. HPS – Following the contour of the sleeve, measure from the HPS to the bottom of the sleeve (including the cuff).
15 ELBOW	Measure across midpoint of sleeve at a right angle to the folded edge.
16 SLEEVE OPENING	With the tape measure at a right angle to the center fold of the sleeve, measure straight across the bottom of the sleeve where it attaches to the cuff.
17 CUFF – HEIGHT	Measure straight down from top to bottom of cuff.
18 CUFF OPENING	Measure straight across the bottom edge of the cuff.
19 SLEEVE PLACKET	a. LENGTH – Measure straight down the sleeve placket without including the cuff. b. WIDTH – Measure straight across the sleeve placket.

(Continues)

©Fairchild Publications, Inc.

HOW TO MEASURE A WOVEN SHIRT

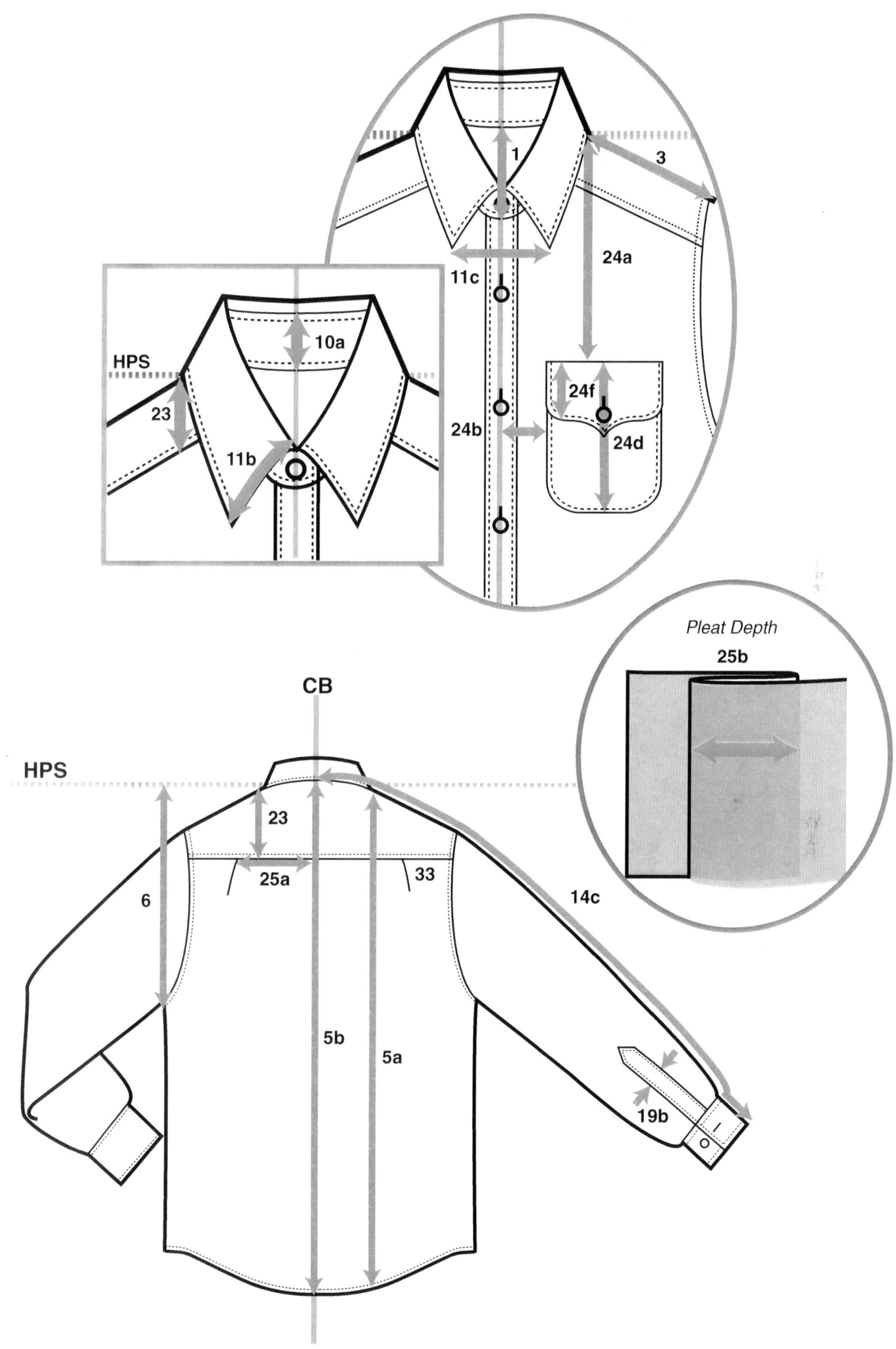

1

3

24a

11c

10a

HPS

23

11b

24b

24f

24d

Pleat Depth

25b

CB

HPS

23

25a

33

14c

6

5b

5a

19b

Illustrated Measurement Points for a Woven Shirt

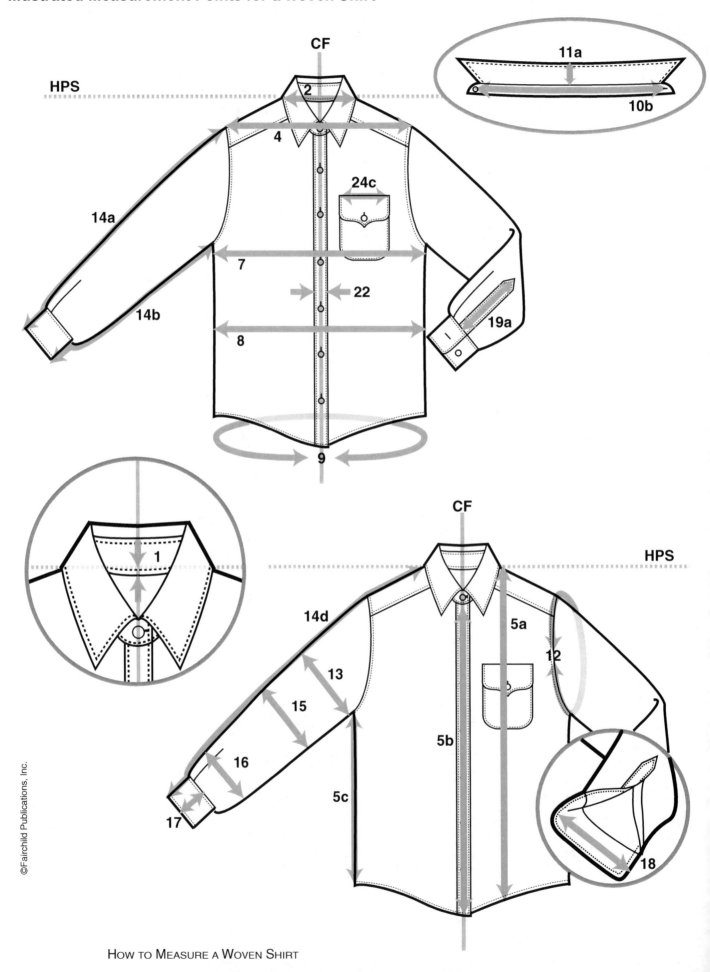

Woven Shirt Spec Sheet

NAME:			DATE:		
SEASON:		STYLE:	SIZE:	LABEL:	
DESCRIPTION:					

FABRICATION:

ACCESSORIES: TRIM:

		FRONT	BACK	TOTAL	COMMENTS
1	NECK DROP				
2	NECK – WIDTH				
3	SHOULDER – LENGTH				
4	ACROSS SHOULDER				
5	LENGTH *				
	a. HPS				
	b. CF/CB				
	c. Side				
6	HPS TO UNDERARM				
7	ACROSS CHEST				
8	ACROSS WAIST				
9	BOTTOM EDGE OPENING (Sweep)				
10	COLLAR BAND				
	a. Height				
	b. Length				
11	COLLAR				
	a. Width - center back				
	b. Width @ point				
	c. Spread				
12	ARMHOLE CIRCUMFERENCE				
13	UPPER SLEEVE – WIDTH				
14	SLEEVE – LENGTH *				
	a. Overarm				
	b. Underarm				
	c. CB				
	d. HPS				
15	ELBOW				
16	SLEEVE OPENING				
17	CUFF – HEIGHT				
18	CUFF OPENING				
19	SLEEVE PLACKET				
	a. Length				
	b. Width				
20	DEPTH OF SLEEVE HEM				
21	BINDING – WIDTH/HEM				
22	FRONT PLACKET – WIDTH				
23	YOKE				
24	POCKET				
	a. Placement – Distance from HPS				
	b. Placement – Distance From CF				
	c. Pocket width				
	d. Pocket length				
	e. Pocket flap width				
	f. Pocket flap length				
25	PLEATS				
	a. Placement - distance from CF/CB				
	b. Depth				
26	DART				
	a. Placement HPS				
	b. Placement CF/CB				
	c. Length of dart				
27	BUTTON PLACEMENT				

REMARKS/OTHER SPECS:

* Circle method for measuring   Abbreviations: high point of shoulder (HPS), center front (CF), center back

How to Measure a Woven Shirt

HOW TO MEASURE A WOVEN SHIRT

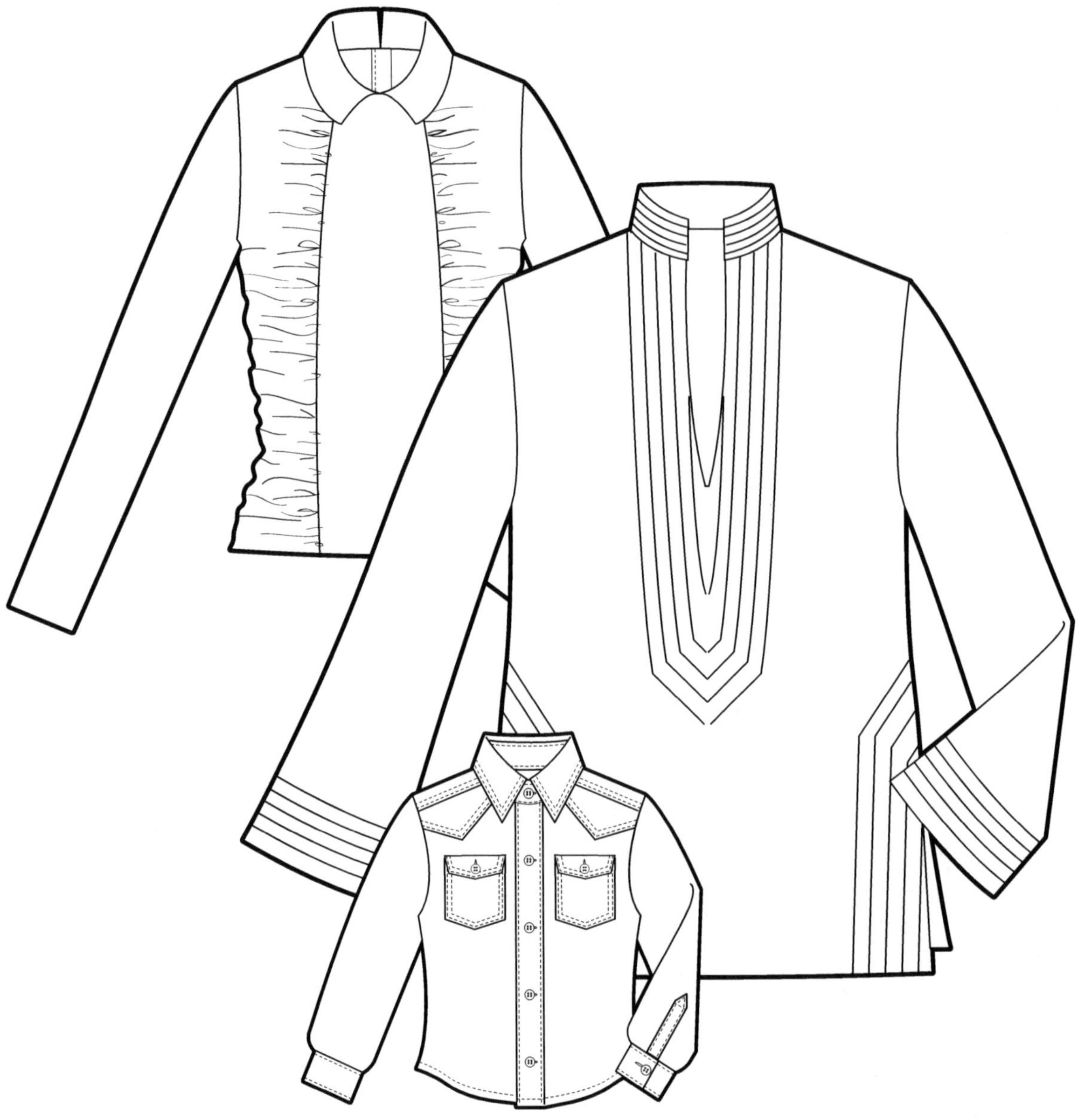

6

1	NECK DROP	BACK – For necklines that scoop below the HPS line measure at center back vertically from the HPS line to neckline. FRONT – Measure down vertically from the HPS at center back to the neckline at center front.
2	NECK – WIDTH	Measure straight across the neckline.
3	FRONT V OPENING	Button vest and fold in half front to back with button side facing you. Measure neck from center back fold following contour edge of neck V to end of front neckline.
4	SHOULDER – LENGTH	Measure along the shoulder seam from the neck seam to the armhole seam.
5	ACROSS SHOULDER	Measure across back from shoulder point (where shoulder seam meets armhole seam) to shoulder point.
6	LENGTH	a. FRONT – Fold buttoned vest in half vertically, measure from CB fold straight down to longest point at vest bottom. b. CB – On vest back measure from CB neckline seam vertically to bottom of garment. c. HPS – On vest back measure from HPS vertically down to bottom of garment. d. Side – Measure the side seam from armhole to bottom of garment. If side seam has slit, measure to where slit begins.
7	HPS TO UNDERARM	Measure from the HPS line to the bottom of the armhole.
8	ARMHOLE	Follow armhole contour from shoulder to bottom of armhole, measuring both front and back.
9	ACROSS CHEST	Measure buttoned garment straight across 1 in., or 2.54 cm, below armhole both front and back.
10	ACROSS WAIST	Measure buttoned garment from side to side, both front and back, at narrowest point. The women's waistline can be located by measuring down 17 in., or 43.18 cm, from the HPS line. Drop 18 in., or 45.72 cm, for men's.
11	POCKET A	a. PLACEMENT – DISTANCE FROM HPS – Measure down vertically from HPS to top edge of pocket. b. PLACEMENT – DISTANCE FROM CF – Measure horizontally from CF to side edge of pocket . c. WIDTH – Measure across top edge of pocket. d. LENGTH – Measure down center of pocket. For irregularly shaped pockets, also measure down side of pockets
12	POCKET B	See #11
13	DART	a. PLACEMENT – DISTANCE FROM HPS – Measure down vertically from HPS to top of dart. b. PLACEMENT – DISTANCE FROM CF – Measure horizontally from CF to dart. c. LENGTH – Measure dart length from top to bottom.
14	BINDING – WIDTH/HEM	Measure straight down to the fold.
15	BOTTOM EDGE OPENING (SWEEP)	Make sure that any pleats or gathers are fully extended, and, following the contour of the hem, measure bottom edge of the garment.
16	BUTTON PLACEMENT	Measure the distance of the center of the first button to the neckline seam. Measure the distance of the center of the first button to the center of the second button. Typically, buttons are evenly spaced thereafter.

Illustrated Measurement Points for a Vest

Vest Spec Sheet

NAME:			DATE:		
SEASON:	STYLE:		SIZE:	LABEL:	
DESCRIPTION:					
FABRICATION:					
ACCESSORIES:				TRIM:	

		FRONT	BACK	TOTAL	COMMENTS
1	NECK DROP				
2	NECK – WIDTH				
3	FRONT – OPENING				
4	SHOULDER – LENGTH				
5	ACROSS SHOULDER				
6	LENGTH*				
	a. Front				
	b. CB				
	c. HPS				
	d. Side				
7	HPS TO UNDERARM				
8	ARMHOLE				
9	ACROSS CHEST				
10	ACROSS WAIST				
11	POCKET A				
	a. Placement – Distance from HPS				
	b. Placement – Distance from CF				
	c. Width				
	d. Length				
12	POCKET B				
	a. Placement – Distance from HPS				
	b. Placement – Distance from CF				
	c. Width				
	d. Length				
13	DART				
	a. Placement – Distance from HPS				
	b. Placement – Distance from CF/CB				
	c. Length				
14	BINDING – WIDTH/HEM				
15	BOTTOM EDGE OPENING (Sweep)				
16	BUTTON PLACEMENT				

REMARKS/OTHER SPECS:

* Circle method for measuring   Abbreviations: high point of shoulder (HPS), center front (CF), center back (

HOW TO MEASURE A VEST

HOW TO MEASURE

A VEST

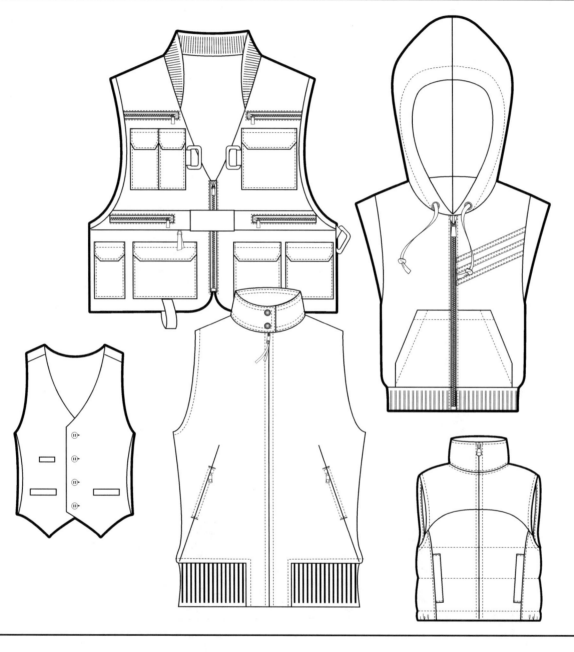

5

©Fairchild Publications, Inc.

18 BELT LOOP	a. PLACEMENT – DISTANCE FROM CF – Measuring from the center of each loop, determine distance of loop to center front.
	b. PLACEMENT – DISTANCE FROM CB – Measuring from the center of each loop, determine distance of loop to center back.
	c. PLACEMENT – DISTANCE FROM SS – Measuring from the center of each loop, determine the distance of loop to the side seam.
	d. WIDTH – Measure horizontally from edge to edge at widest point.
	e. LENGTH – Measure vertically from end to end including overlap.
19 DART	a. PLACEMENT – DISTANCE FROM CF – Measure from center front to dart edge.
	b. PLACEMENT – DISTANCE FROM CB – Measure from center back to dart edge.
	c. LENGTH – Measure from waistline to dart ending point.
	d. DEPTH – Measure dart depth at widest point by feeling through the fabric.
20 HEM – DEPTH	Measure top edge of hem vertically to bottom fold.
21 CUFF – HEIGHT	Measure vertically from top to bottom of cuff.
22 YOKE	a. PLACEMENT – CF/CB – Measure down center front/center back from garment waistline seam to bottom of yoke.
	b. PLACEMENT – SS – Measure down side seam from garment waistline seam to bottom of yoke.
23 BUTTON PLACEMENT	Button on waistband is centered above zipper placket. For extension waistband, determine the extension by measuring from center of the button to edge of fold.

1	WAISTLINE SEAM PLACEMENT	Measure distance from garment waistline seam to natural waist.
2	WAISTLINE SEAM CIRCUMFERENCE	a. RELAXED – Measure across center of waistband from side to side, both front and back.
		b. EXTENDED – Measure as above with elastic fully extended.
3	WAISTBAND – HEIGHT	Measure width from top of waistband vertically down to waistline seam.
4	HIGH HIP	Locate the high hip position by dropping down 4 in., or 10.16 cm, from natural waist; measure from side seam to side seam, both front and back. For low rise pants, subtract drop from natural waist to garment waistline seam (see #1). For Hollywood waist, add rise from natural waist to garment waistline seam (see #1).
5	LOW HIP	Locate the low hip position* by dropping down 7 in., or 17.78 cm, from natural waist. Measure from side seam to side seam, both front and back. For low rise pants, subtract drop from natural waist to garment waistline seam (see #1). For Hollywood waist, add rise from natural waist to garment waistline seam (see #1).
		* Low hip positions for other categories: Juniors, Petites, Plus: measure as above; girls and boys: measure up 2.5 in., or 5.461 cm, from crotch; mens: measure up 3 in., or 7.62 cm, from crotch.
6	RISE	Measure from the crotch (the point where the rise seam intersects the inseam). Follow the contour of the rise seam to the waistline seam.
7	INSEAM	Measure from the crotch (the point where the rise seam intersects the inseam), following inseam down to bottom of pant opening.
8	OUTSEAM	Measure from waistline seam down, following the side seam contour to the bottom of the pant leg.
9	THIGH CIRCUMFERENCE	Measure thigh inseam down 1 in., or 2.54 cm, below the crotch. At this point, measure across pant leg from inseam to side seam, both front and back.
10	KNEE CIRCUMFERENCE	For womenswear, determine the knee position* by measuring thigh inseam down 12 in., or 30.48 cm, below the crotch. At this point, measure across leg from side seam to side seam both front and back.
		* Knee positions for other categories: Petites: 11 in., or 27.94 cm, Plus Size: 13 in., or 33.02 cm, Junior: 12 in., or 30.48 cm, Boys/Girls: 1.5 in., or 3.81 cm, less than half the finished inseam length; Mens: 2 in., or 5.08 cm, less than half the finished inseam length.
11	ANKLE CIRCUMFERENCE/ BOTTOM EDGE	Measure the bottom edge from side seam to side seam both front and back.
12	ZIPPER PLACKET	a. WIDTH – Measure from open edge of placket to placket stitching line.
		b. LENGTH – Measure perpendicularly from waistband seam down opening to bottom of placket.
13	POCKET A	a. PLACEMENT – WAISTLINE SEAM – Measure vertically down from waistline seam to top of pocket edge.
		b. PLACEMENT – CF – Measure horizontally across from center front to top and bottom of pocket edge.
		c. PLACEMENT – SIDE SEAM – Measure horizontally across from side seam to top and bottom of pocket edge.
		d. PLACEMENT – CB – Measure horizontally across from center back to top and bottom of pocket edge.
		e. WIDTH – Measure across the top of the pocket.
		f. LENGTH – Measure down the center of the pocket. For irregularly shaped pockets, take a second measurement down the side edge of the pocket.
14	POCKET B	See #13
15	POCKET C	See #13
16	POCKET D	See #13
17	PLEAT	a. PLACEMENT – Measure from center front to outside edge of pleat.
		b. DEPTH – Tuck tape measure into pleat and measure the depth.

(Continues)

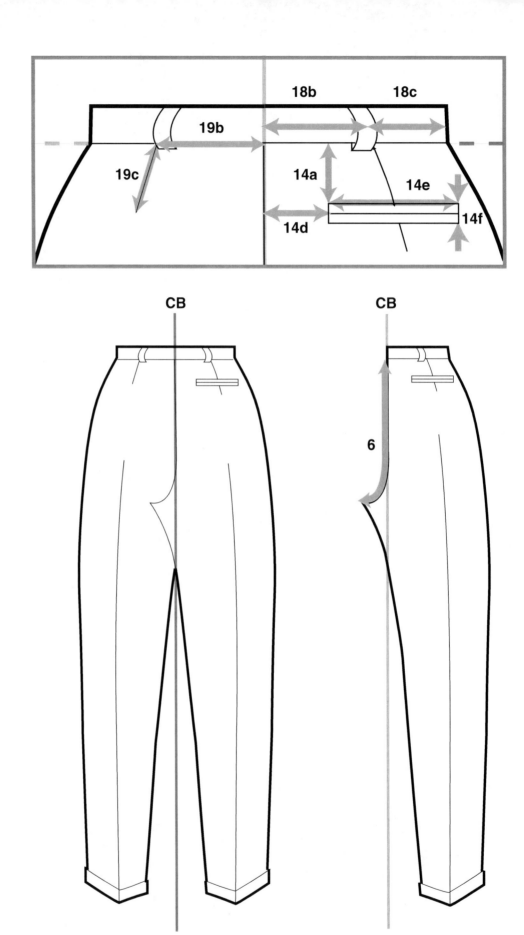

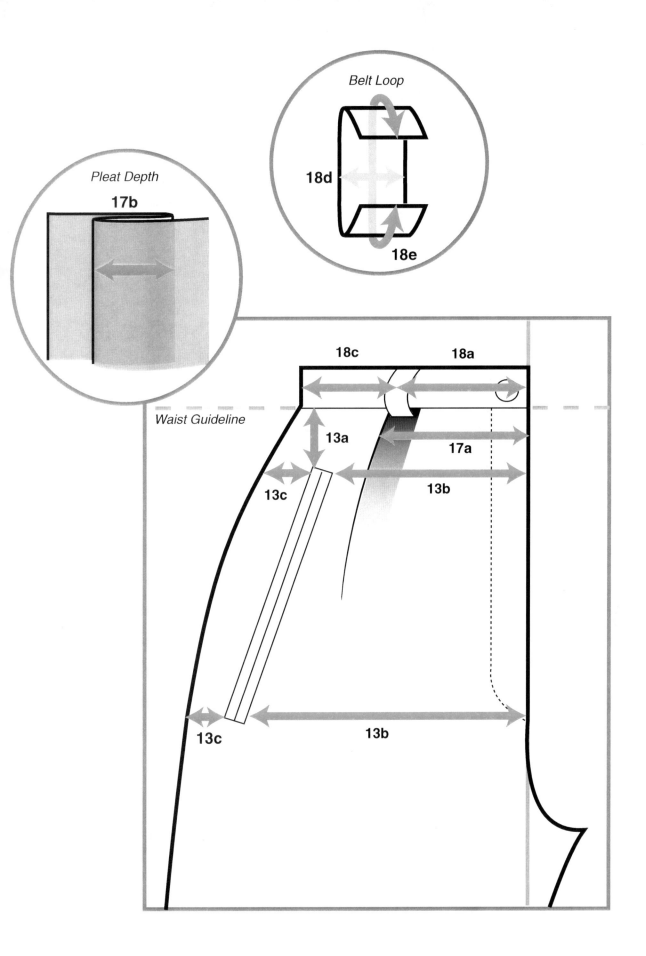

Pleat Depth

17b

Belt Loop

18d

18e

18c   **18a**

Waist Guideline

13a

17a

13c

13b

13c

13b

Illustrated Measurement Points for Pants and Shorts

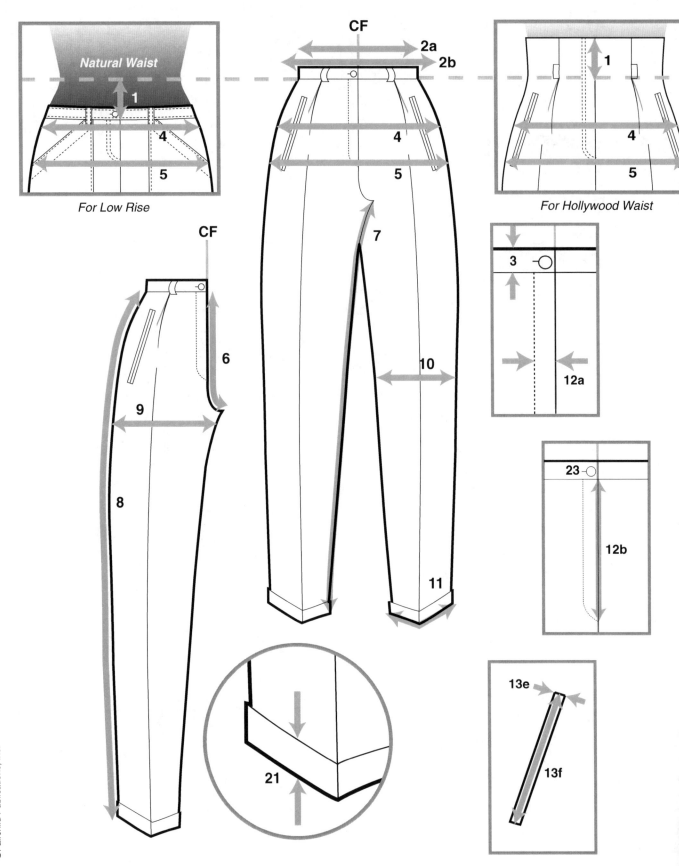

Natural Waist

For Low Rise

CF

For Hollywood Waist

CF

Pants and Shorts Spec Sheet

NAME:			DATE:	
SEASON:	STYLE:		SIZE:	LABEL:
DESCRIPTION:				

FABRICATION:

ACCESSORIES: TRIM:

		FRONT	BACK	TOTAL	COMMENTS
1	WAISTLINE SEAM PLACEMENT above/below natural waist*				
2	WAISTLINE SEAM CIRCUMFERENCE				
	a. Relaxed				
	b. Extended				
3	WAISTBAND – HEIGHT				
4	HIGH HIP (4 in., or 10.16 cm, from natural waist)				
5	LOW HIP (7 in., or 17.78 cm, from natural waist)				
6	RISE				
7	INSEAM				
8	OUTSEAM				
9	THIGH CIRCUMFERENCE				
10	KNEE CIRCUMFERENCE				
11	ANKLE CIRCUMFERENCE				
12	ZIPPER PLACKET				
	a. Width				
	b. Length				
13	POCKET A				
	a. Placement – Waistline seam to top pocket edge				
	b. Placement – CF to pocket edge (top/bottom)				
	c. Placement – Side seam to pocket edge (top/bottom)				
	d. Placement – CB to pocket edge (top/bottom)				
	e. Pocket width				
	f. Pocket length				
14	POCKET B				
	a. Placement – Waistline seam to top pocket edge				
	b. Placement – CF to pocket edge (top/bottom)				
	c. Placement – Side seam to pocket edge (top/bottom)				
	d. Placement – CB to pocket edge (top/bottom)				
	e. Pocket width				
	f. Pocket length				
15	POCKET C				
	a. Placement – Waistline seam to top pocket edge				
	b. Placement – CF to pocket edge (top/bottom)				
	c. Placement – Side seam to pocket edge (top/bottom)				
	d. Placement – CB to pocket edge (top/bottom)				
	e. Pocket width				
	f. Pocket length				
16	POCKET D				
	a. Placement – Waistline seam to top pocket edge				
	b. Placement – CF to pocket edge (top/bottom)				
	c. Placement – Side seam to pocket edge (top/bottom)				
	d. Placement – CB to pocket edge (top/bottom)				
	e. Pocket width				
	f. Pocket length				
17	PLEAT				
	a. Placement – Distance from CF				
	b. Pleat depth				
18	BELT LOOP				
	a. Placement – Distance from CF				
	b. Distance from CB				
	c. Distance from SS				
	d. Belt loop width				
	e. Belt loop length				
19	DART				
	a. Placement – Distance from CF				
	b. Placement – Distance from CB				
	c. Dart length				
	d. Dart depth				
20	HEM – DEPTH				
21	CUFF – HEIGHT				
22	YOKE				
	a. Placement – Waistline seam to yoke @ CF/CB				
	b. Placement – Waistline seam to yoke @ SS				
23	BUTTON PLACEMENT				

REMARKS/OTHER SPECS:

* Circle method for measuring   Abbreviations: center front (CF), center back (CB), side seam

©Fairchild Publications, Inc.

HOW TO MEASURE PANTS AND SHORTS

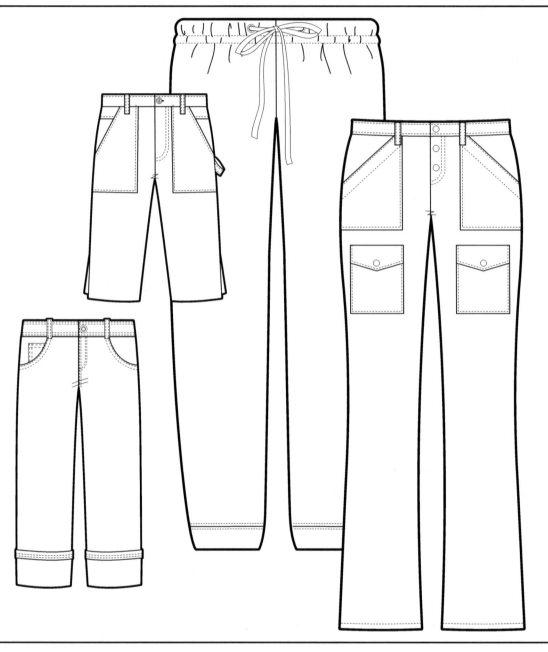

Table of Measurement Points for a Skirt

1 WAISTLINE SEAM PLACEMENT	Measure distance from garment waistline seam to natural waist.
2 WAISTLINE SEAM CIRCUMFERENCE	a. RELAXED – Measure across center of waistband from side to side, both front and back. b. EXTENDED – Measure waist as above with elastic fully extended.
3 WAISTBAND – HEIGHT	Measure width from top of waistband vertically down to waistline seam.
4 HIGH HIP	Dropping down 4 in., or 10.16 cm, from natural waist, measure high hip from side seam to side seam, both front and back. For skirts that sit on the hip, subtract drop from natural waist to garment waistline seam (see #1). For Hollywood waist, add rise from natural waist to garment waistline seam (see #1).
5 LOW HIP	Dropping down 7 in., or 17.78 cm, from natural waist, measure low hip from side seam to side seam, both front and back. For skirts that sit on the hip, subtract drop from natural waist to garment waistline seam (see #1). For Hollywood waist, add rise from natural waist to garment waistline seam (see #1).
6 LENGTH	a. CF/CB – Measure down center from waistline seam to bottom edge. b. SIDE – Following the contour of the side seam, measure down from waistline seam to bottom edge.
7 SWEEP	Making sure that any pleats or gathers are fully extended, follow the contour of the hem and measure bottom edge of the garment.
8 SLIT	a. LENGTH – Measure length of slit opening from the highest point of the slit to the hem. b. DEPTH – Measure horizontally across the slit from opening edge of slit to the end point of the overlap.
9 DART	a. PLACEMENT CF/CB – Measure from center front/center back to dart edge. b. LENGTH – Measure from waistline seam to dart ending point. c. DEPTH – Measure dart depth at widest point by feeling through the fabric.
10 POCKET A	a. PLACEMENT – WAISTLINE – Measure vertically down waistline seam to pocket edge. b. PLACEMENT – CF – Measure horizontally to top and bottom of pocket edge. c. PLACEMENT – SIDE SEAM – Measure horizontally across to top and bottom of pocket edge. d. PLACEMENT – CB – Measure horizontally to top and bottom of pocket edge. e. WIDTH – Measure across the top of the pocket. f. LENGTH – Measure down the center of the pocket. For irregularly shaped pockets, take a second measurement down the side of the pocket.
11 POCKET B	See #11
12 PLEAT	a. PLACEMENT – CF – Measure to outside edge of pleat. b. DEPTH – Tuck tape measure into pleat and measure the depth.
13 ZIPPER PLACKET	a. WIDTH – Measure from open edge of placket to placket stitching line. b. LENGTH – Measure from center front of waistline seam vertically down opening to bottom of placket.
14 BELT LOOP	a. PLACEMENT – CF – Measuring from the center of the loop, determine distance of loop to center front. b. PLACEMENT – CENTER BACK – Measuring from the center of the loop, determine distance of loop to center back. c. PLACEMENT – SIDE SEAM – Measuring from the center of the loop, determine the distance of the loop to the side seam. d. WIDTH – Measure horizontally from edge to edge at widest point. e. LENGTH – Measure vertically from end to end including overlap.
15 HEM – DEPTH	Measure top edge of hem vertically to bottom fold.
16 BUTTON PLACEMENT	Button on waistband is centered above zipper placket. For extension waistband, determine the extension by measuring from center of the button to edge of fold.

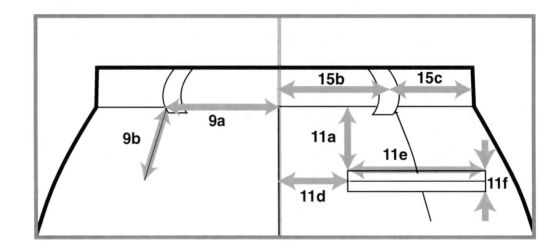

CB

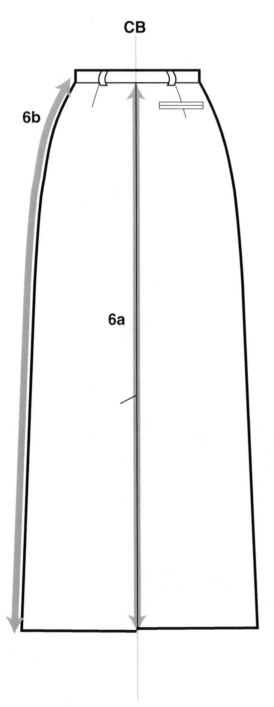

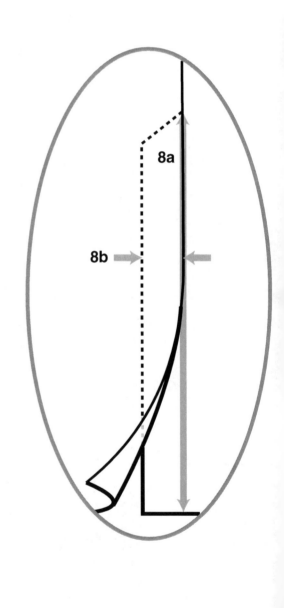

HOW TO MEASURE A SKIRT

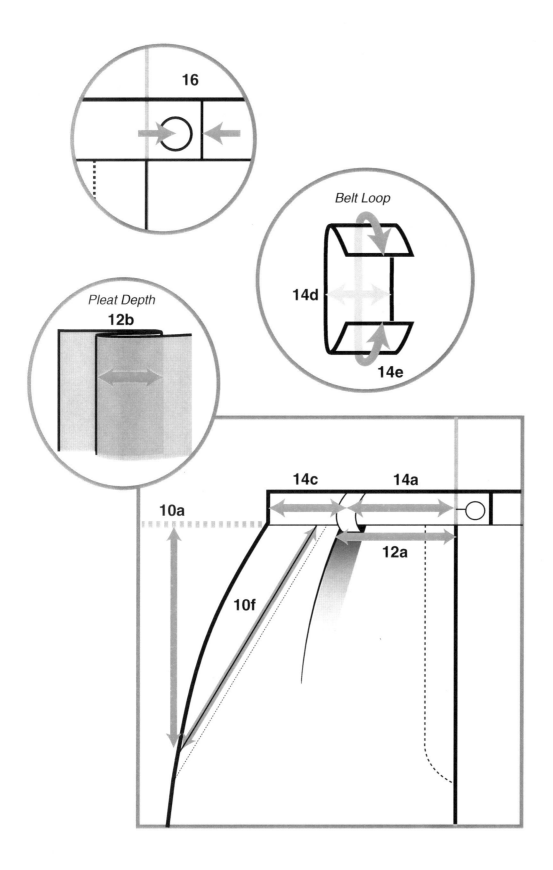

16

Belt Loop

14d

14e

Pleat Depth

12b

14c   14a

10a

10f

12a

Illustrated Measurement Points for Pants and Shorts

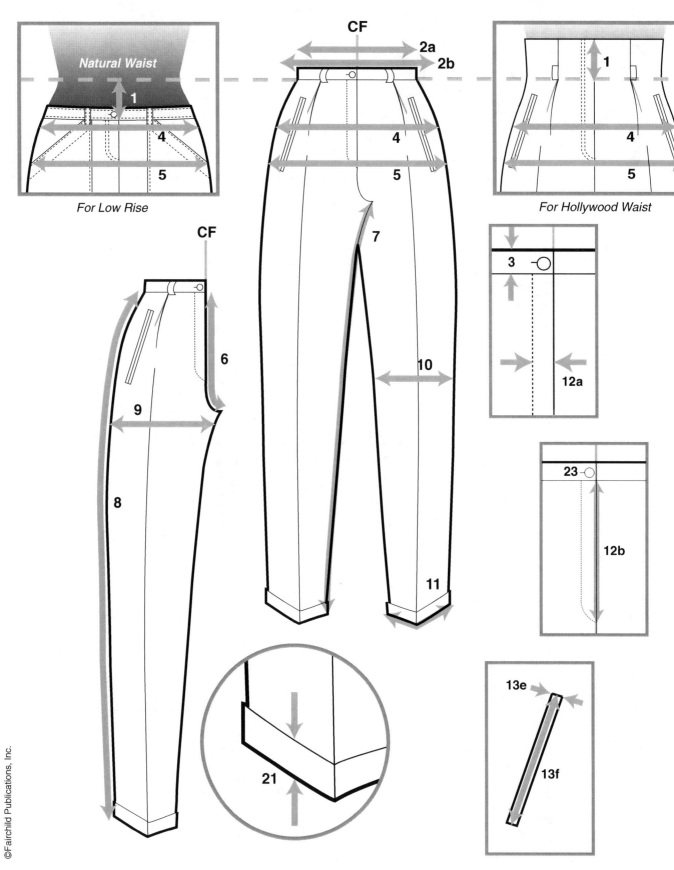

Natural Waist

CF

2a

2b

For Low Rise

For Hollywood Waist

CF

Skirt Spec Sheet

NAME:			DATE:		
SEASON:		STYLE:	SIZE:	LABEL:	
DESCRIPTION:					
FABRICATION:					
ACCESSORIES:				TRIM:	

		FRONT	BACK	TOTAL	COMMENTS
1	WAISTLINE SEAM PLACEMENT– above/below natural waist*				
2	WAISTLINE SEAM CIRCUMFERENCE				
	a. Relaxed				
	b. Extended				
3	WAISTBAND – HEIGHT				
4	HIGH HIP (4 in., or 10.16 cm, from natural waist)				
5	LOW HIP (7 in., or 17.78 cm, from natural waist)				
6	LENGTH				
	a. CF/CB				
	b. Side				
7	SWEEP				
8	SLIT				
	a. Length				
	b. Depth				
9	DART				
	a. Placement – CF/CB				
	b. Length				
	c. Depth				
10	POCKET A				
	a. Placement – Waist line seam to top pocket edge				
	b. Placement – CF to pocket edge (top/bottom)				
	c. Placement – Side seam to pocket edge (top/bottom)				
	d. Placement – CB to pocket edge (top/bottom)				
	e. Pocket width				
	f. Pocket length				
11	POCKET B				
	a. Placement – Waist line seam to top pocket edge				
	b. Placement – CF to pocket edge (top/bottom)				
	c. Placement – Side seam to pocket edge (top/bottom)				
	d. Placement – CB to pocket edge (top/bottom)				
	e. Pocket width				
	f. Pocket length				
12	PLEAT				
	a. Placement – Distance from CF				
	b. Depth				
13	ZIPPER PLACKET				
	a. Width				
	b. Length				
14	BELT LOOP				
	a. Placement – Distance from CF				
	b. Placement – Distance from CB				
	c. Placement – Distance from SS				
	d. Width				
	e. Length				
15	HEM – DEPTH				
16	BUTTON PLACEMENT				

REMARKS/OTHER SPECS:

* Circle method for measuring   Abbreviations: high point of shoulder (HPS), center front (CF), center back (CB), side seam (SS)

©Fairchild Publications, Inc.

HOW TO MEASURE A SKIRT

FRONT AND BACK VIEW CROQUIS FIGURES

FRONT AND BACK VIEW CROQUIS FIGURES

FRONT AND BACK VIEW CROQUIS FIGURES

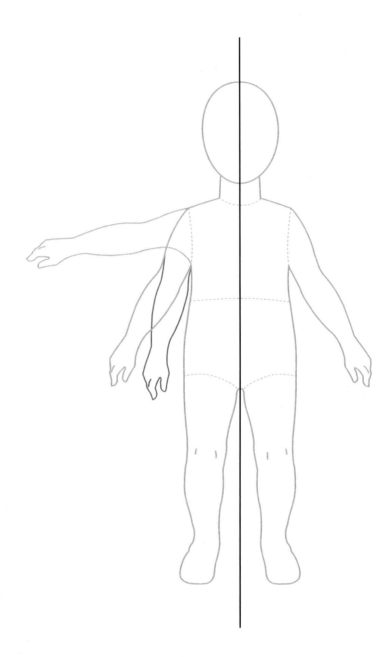

FRONT AND BACK VIEW CROQUIS FIGURES

FRONT AND BACK VIEW CROQUIS FIGURES

FRONT AND BACK VIEW CROQUIS FIGURES

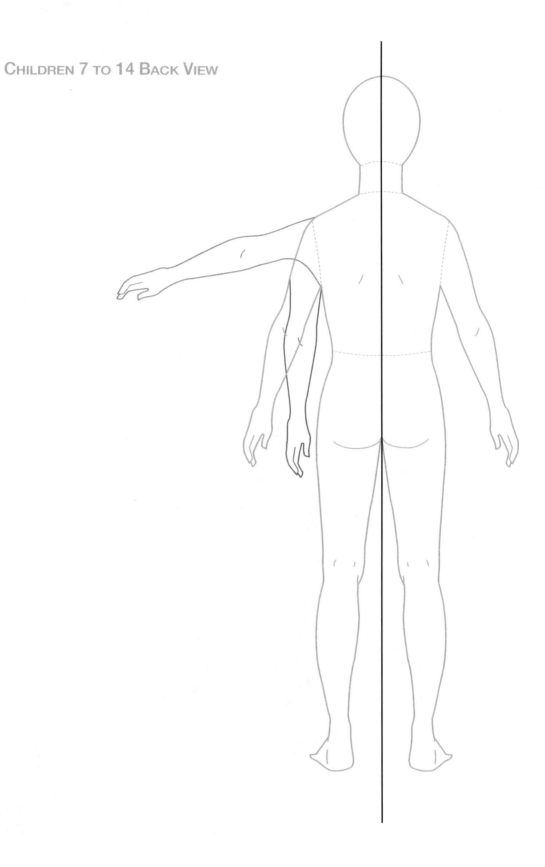

FRONT AND BACK VIEW CROQUIS FIGURES

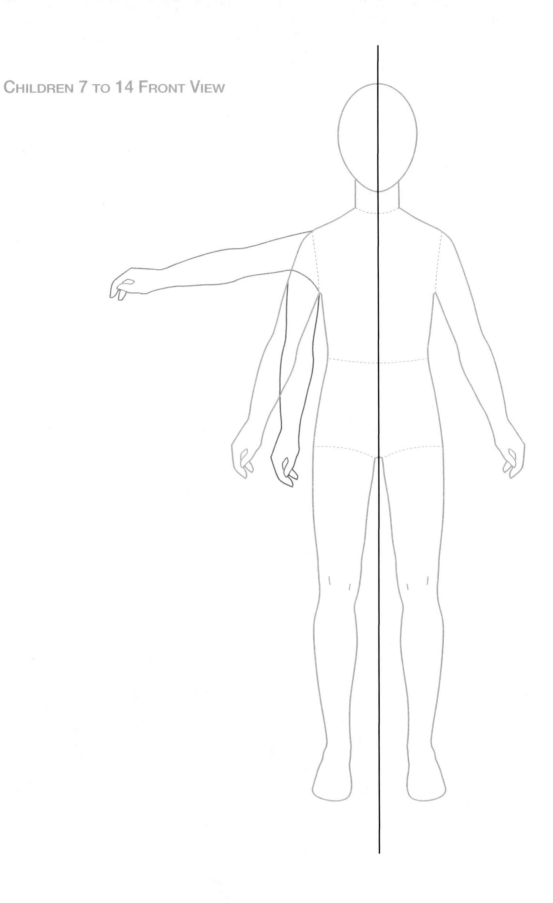

FRONT AND BACK VIEW CROQUIS FIGURES

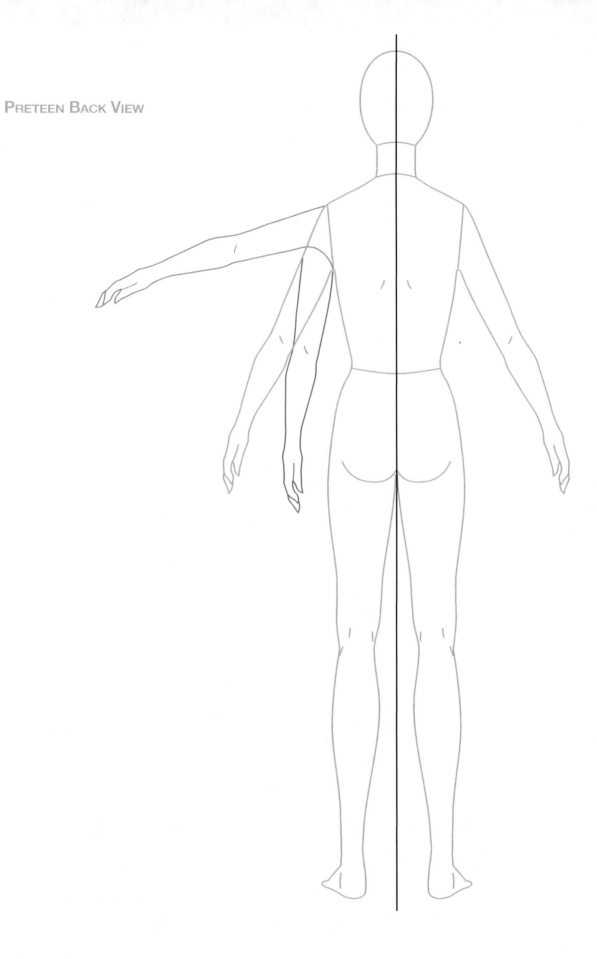

FRONT AND BACK VIEW CROQUIS FIGURES

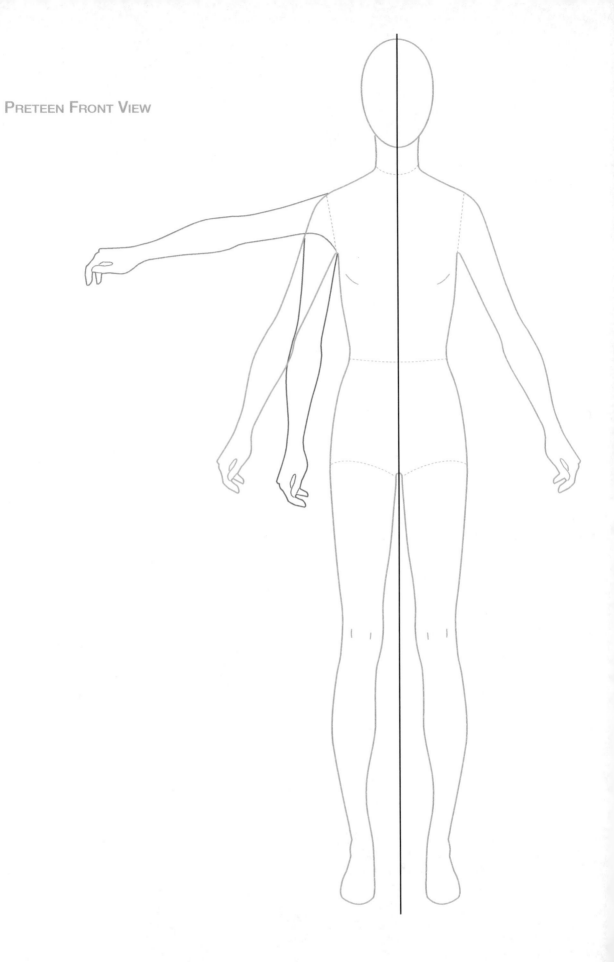

FRONT AND BACK VIEW CROQUIS FIGURES

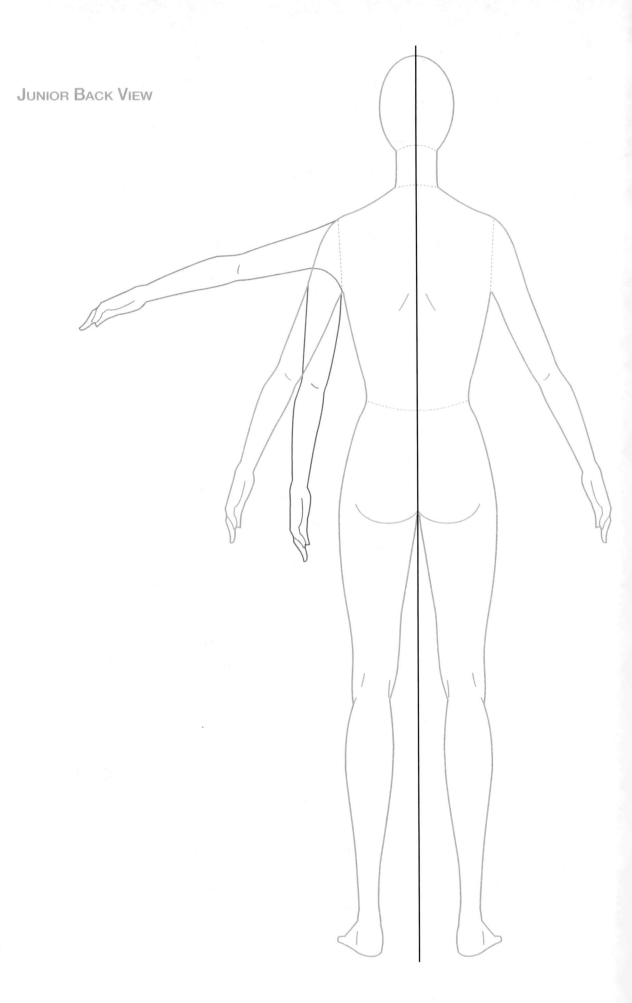

JUNIOR BACK VIEW

FRONT AND BACK VIEW CROQUIS FIGURES

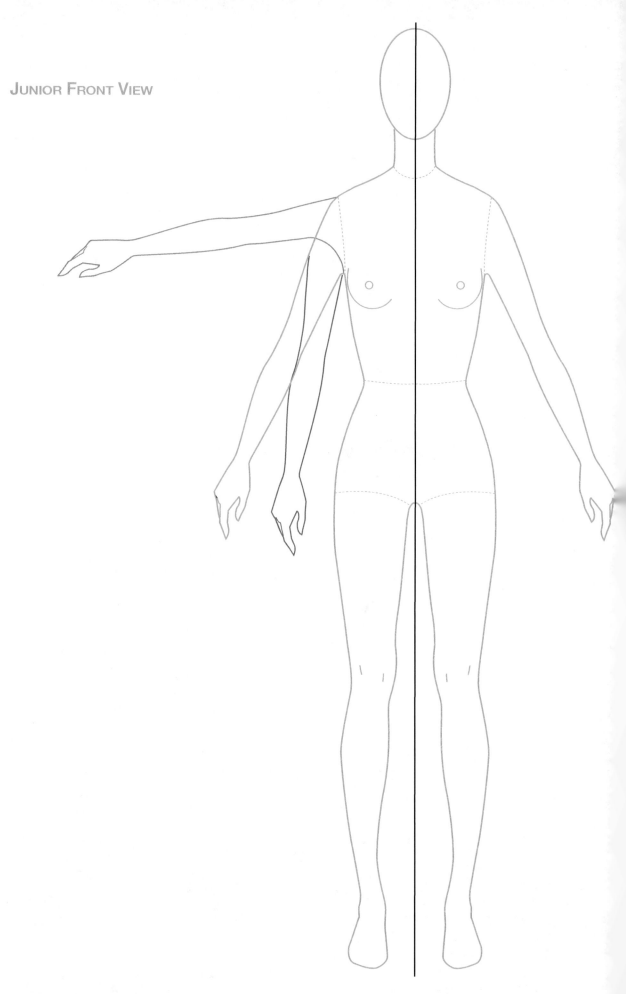

FRONT AND BACK VIEW CROQUIS FIGURES

MEN'S BACK VIEW

FRONT AND BACK VIEW CROQUIS FIGURES

MEN'S FRONT VIEW

©Fairchild Publications, Inc.

FRONT AND BACK VIEW CROQUIS FIGURES

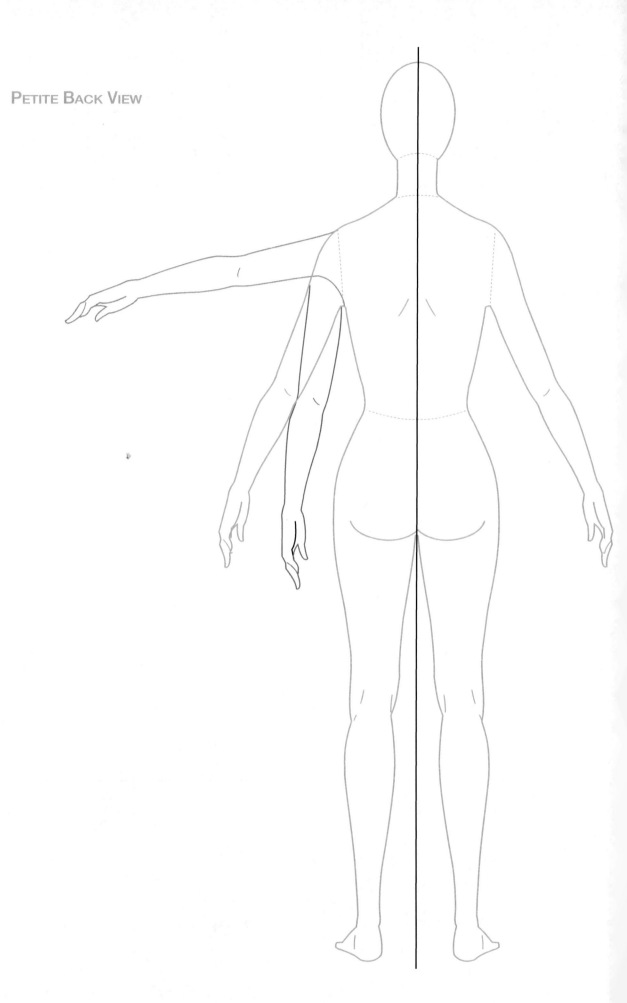

FRONT AND BACK VIEW CROQUIS FIGURES

PETITE FRONT VIEW

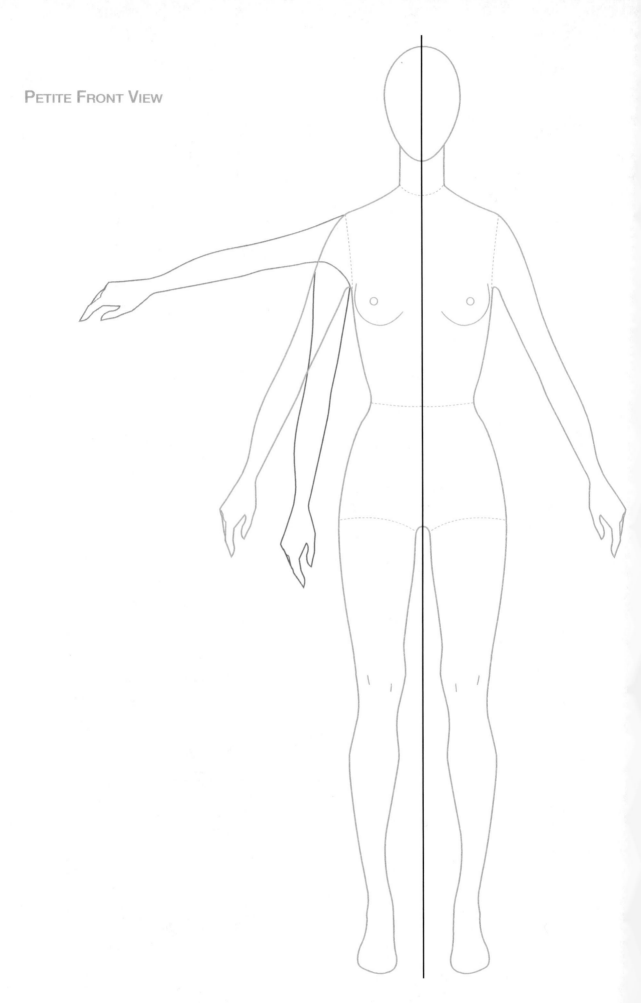

FRONT AND BACK VIEW CROQUIS FIGURES

FRONT AND BACK VIEW CROQUIS FIGURES

PLUS SIZE FRONT VIEW

FRONT AND BACK VIEW CROQUIS FIGURES

FRONT AND BACK VIEW CROQUIS FIGURES

MISSY FRONT VIEW

FRONT AND BACK VIEW CROQUIS FIGURES

FRONT AND BACK VIEW

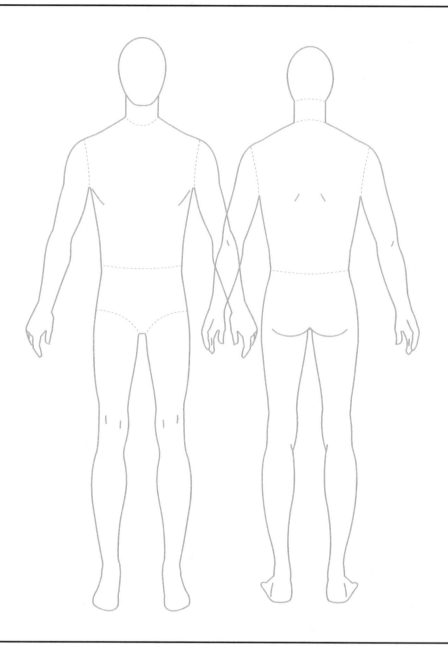

These flat sketches were built to facilitate color/pattern blocking and can be filled using the group selection tool.

METHODS FOR DATA ENTRY USING THE CD-ROM

■ As mentioned, you can simply print out the spec sheets and grading worksheet for manual record keeping.

■ Depending on your access to Microsoft Excel, you can open the appropriate file from the Excel spec sheets folder and, referring to the diagrams in the text, enter the measurements for your garment on the computer. This edition of *The Spec Manual* includes Excel spec sheets that automatically calculate the sum of front and back measurements when a total circumference is required. The programmed cells in the TOTAL Column will read 0.00 until front and back values are entered. Excel works on the decimal system and the Fraction to Decimal Conversion Chart (Appendix E) has been included for this purpose.

You can post your Excel specs to a local network or password protected Web site where third party software (e.g., Worksheet-Server™) allows live data sharing. In this way, changes cannot occur without being visible to everyone involved in a collaborative workgroup.

- As mentioned, you can simply view and print the figures, spec sheets, grading worksheet, clip art, and graphs for manual drawing and data entry.

- Depending on your digital drawing skills, you can import the appropriate croquis figure into a drawing program (e.g., Adobe Illustrator). The croquis figures are included on the CD-ROM as individual files in the "Croquis Figures" folder. First launch your drawing program and then open the croquis file that you need. The figure and alternate arm positions are on three separate locked layers. With the "Flat Sketch" layer active, sketch half of your garment using the pen tool. Select your half flat sketch, then reflect and copy to create a symmetrical flat.

  If you are working in Adobe Illustrator, *The Spec Manual* brush library of stitches and trims may be imported by going to Window>Other Library and opening the file BrushStitchLibrary.ai. Using this brush library and the clip art featured on the CD-ROM, quickly add stitching, trim, and accessories. Describe intricate details with exploded views. For storyboard presentations that do not require garment specs, take advantage of the layers feature in your drawing program by including technical information on a separate layer hidden from view. Similarly, the croquis layers can also be unlocked and then hidden or discarded entirely. By applying colors and patterns to your flats, you can illustrate how a final garment will look.

- If you have access to both a printer and a scanner, you can print out the appropriate croquis figure and manually sketch a "rough" of your garment. Then scan the rough and open the image in a drawing program (e.g., Adobe Illustrator). With the background layer active, choose Template from the Layers palette menu. Template layers will not print or export. Create a new layer and finish your sketch using the pen tool. When you have completed the drawing, you can either hide or discard the "rough" template layer for onscreen presentation. Working this way facilitates a free flow of ideas for designers who are less inclined to sketch directly on the computer. Archive your work and, over time, build a custom flats library.

- Although grids are featured in the preferences of many drawing programs, none of the guides actually print. Printable graph files for both inches and centimeters are included the Clip Art Library folder. In a drawing program, open one of the graph files and, having completed data entry on your spec sheet, plot the measurements with each square representing 1 inch or 1 centimeter on your garment.

- You can also use one of the flat sketches arranged by size category in the Clip Art Library folder. Launch your drawing application and open the file you need (a directory for these sketches is featured in Chapter 14). Modify or use as is.

provided) in a Web-based architecture, collaborative work groups can share and manage data with a standard HTML browser.

REQUIREMENTS FOR MAC AND PC

The Spec Manual CD-ROM contains files in PDF and Excel formats. Acrobat Reader is the software you need to view and print the clip art library, figures, and graphs.

The minimum system requirements for Acrobat Reader 7.0 are:

Windows

- Intel® Pentium® processor

- Microsoft® Windows 2000 with Service Pack 2, Windows XP Professional or Home Edition, or Windows XP Tablet PC Edition

- 128 MB of RAM

- Up to 90 MB of available hard-disk space

- Microsoft Internet Explorer 5.5 or higher

- CD-ROM drive (or compatible DVD-ROM drive) for installation

Macintosh

- PowerPC® G3 processor

- Mac OS X v.10.2.8 or 10.3

- Up to 35 MB of RAM

- Up to 125 MB of available hard-disk space

- CD-ROM drive (or compatible DVD-ROM drive) for installation

E-MAIL

E-mail is an essential communications tool in the global supply chain. Most file formats can be e-mailed as attachments. Keep in mind that the recipient of your e-mail must have the appropriate application to view your attachments. An option is to save your flat sketch as a PDF in Illustrator or Photoshop. When you send a PDF file as an attachment, provide the recipient with a link to Acrobat Reader. When you send an Excel spec sheet as an attachment, provide the recipient with Microsoft Excel Viewer, a small size freeware that allows for the viewing and printing of Excel workbooks.

CF — Center Front

CB — Center Back

HPS — High Point of Shoulder

SS — Side Seam

GENERAL GUIDELINES FOR MEASURING GARMENTS

1. Always use a fabric or plastic tape measure. Occasionally, check your tape against a metal ruler for accuracy.

2. All measurements should be taken with the garment lying in a natural position on a flat surface. Gently smooth out all wrinkles.

3. Close all buttons and zippers (unless otherwise indicated) before you measure the garment.

4. When measuring a seam with a curved contour, stand the tape measure on its end for the most accurate measurement.

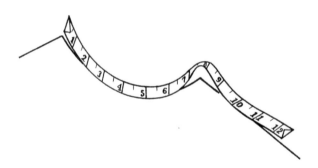

Using the CD-ROM

Your computer skills and access to hardware and applications will determine how you use the CD-ROM. Given modest skills and a minimum computer configuration, you can print out the files for the figures, spec sheets, grading worksheet, and clip art and then work with them manually. With access to a drawing program (not provided), you can use the croquis figures to create digital sketches. The spec sheets are interactive forms that you can use with a spreadsheet program (not provided) for digital data entry and storage. The Excel spec sheets automatically calculate the sum of front and back measurements when a total circumference is called for. It is also possible to post your flat sketches and spec sheets to an internal network or a password protected Web site for real time communication among multiple users. Using third-party software (not

Using the Spec Sheets

The spec sheet templates are included as hard copy in the text and in digital format on the CD-ROM.

Find the spec sheet that comes closest to the silhouette you require (e.g., for a half-slip, use the skirt spec sheet, for a full slip use the dress spec sheet; for boxer shorts, use the pant spec sheet; and so on).

All the forms, illustrations, and tables are cross-referenced with the same numbers within respective chapters. The drawings and tables show you exactly where and how to measure the garment.

The garments diagrammed in *The Spec Manual* have a wide variety of design details. However, in some cases a numbered measurement point that is included on the spec sheet and table is left out of a diagram because the garment illustrated does not feature that particular design detail. For consistency, all garments are illustrated right side out. When a measurement is taken on the inside of the garment, you will not see it on the diagram.

Enter your data in the columns marked "FRONT," "BACK," AND "TOTAL." A fourth column labeled "COMMENTS" is for miscellaneous information. Standard industry practice requires the sum of front and back measurements for certain garment details. Consult the Illustrated Measurement Points for your garment to determine if a total measurement is necessary.

Fill in all the blanks on the spec sheets. If the garment being measured does not feature all the design details itemized on the spec sheet, record "N/A" (Not Applicable) or fill the corresponding cell with a gray tone. That way, all parties concerned will know the omission is by design and not oversight.

If the garment being measured has design details that are not itemized on the spec sheet, list those points of measurement in the box reserved for "Remarks/Other Specs." Be sure to specify stitching information (e.g., single or double needle, merro, zigzag and bar tacks). It is helpful to feature "exploded" views of more intricate design details in your flat sketch.

Methods of measuring can vary from one company to another. When there is more than one method for taking a measurement, it is important to determine the measurement criteria for your company and to specifically indicate the method used on your spec sheet.

A key to the abbreviations used is featured on all the spec sheets directly below "Remarks/Other Specs."

Both front and back croquis figures have three arm positions. The arm position closest to the body corresponds to a set-in sleeve on a tailored jacket. The most extended arm position is best for garments with raglan and drop shoulder armholes as well as kimono and dolman sleeves. The middle arm position is appropriate for all other needs.

The legs on the croquis figures are shoulder width apart. Fabric drape is determined by gravity, so the fullness of a garment should be indicated in the center of the garment.

You can also adapt one of the croquis figures to approximate your fit model. Apparel production is geared to a specific market demographic. The importance of determining body measurements for your target customer cannot be overly stressed. Whereas runway models epitomize the fantasy of fashion, fit models represent a perfect sample size for a specific market and are employed for an important reality check. Once you have found a suitable fit model, measure the body using the following landmarks and circumferences:

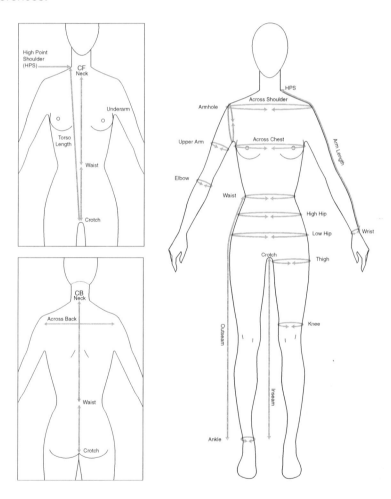

For more information about standard body measurements go to www.sizeusa.com and www.astm.com.

- ■ **Sample Spec Sheets and Garment Graphs.** These are for skirts, pants, vests, shirts, bodysuits, sweaters, tailored jackets, and outerwear. Chapter 13 contains garment graphs of charted measurements based on sample spec sheets. Measurement points on the spec sheets have been newly ordered for this edition to facilitate the graphing of garments.

- ■ **Clip Art Library.** This includes flats for all garment and size categories that were created using *The Spec Manual* croquis figures. Chapter 14 includes more than 100 flats and additional clip art for collars, pockets, accessories, trim, and stitches.

- ■ **Button Selector Gauge**

- ■ **Graph Templates in Inches and Centimeters**

- ■ **Metric Conversion Chart**

- ■ **Fraction-to-Decimal Conversion Chart**

- ■ **Grading Worksheet.** This is a template that can be used in tandem with incremental grade guides (Appendix G) to record graded measurements as well as color and size assortment for counter samples. Appendix F contains a grading worksheet that, along with a completed spec sheet and sketch, can be used to create a comprehensive spec pack for all garment categories.

- ■ **Incremental Grade Guides.** These are for calculating graded measurements. Appendix G includes tables for all size categories.

- ■ **CD-ROM.** This has croquis figures, spec sheet templates, a clip art library, a grading worksheet template, and printable graphs.

Using the Croquis Figures

The croquis figures are included in the text as hard copy and in digital format on the CD-ROM. They are sized to allow for sketching even the smallest garment details and have a relative proportion to one another. Keep in mind that if you use more than one size category in a presentation (e.g., children 4–6x with 7–14) the figures should be uniformly scaled to maintain their size relationship.

Select the croquis figure that most closely matches your target customer's size category. All croquis figures represent the body measurements for the sample size for each category. When you flat sketch on these figures, the result is a precise illustration of your garment drawn to scale. The more accurate your sketch, the more accurate your first sample.

Introduction

A specification manual is a guide for measuring and record keeping that reflects standard garment industry practices. It is a tool for designers, merchandisers, pattern makers, and suppliers who measure garments. *The Spec Manual* consists of the following:

■ **Front and Back View Croquis Figures.** These are provided so that your flat sketches will have a unified and relative proportion. Chapter Two contains croquis figures for missy, petite, plus size, men, juniors, preteen, children 7 to 14, children 4 to 6x, toddlers, and 1-year olds.

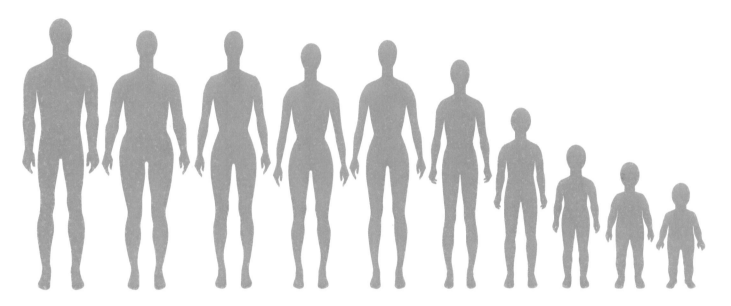

■ **Spec Sheet Templates.** These are for skirts, pants, vests, shirts, bodysuits, sweaters, tailored jackets, outerwear, and bras. Chapters 3 to 12 contain forms that can be used for documenting the measurements of developmental, meeting approval, and production samples.

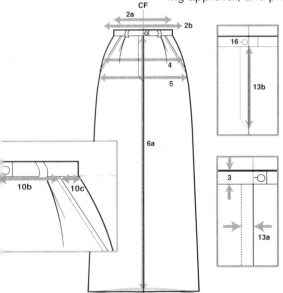

■ **Illustrated Measurement Points.** These are given for skirts, pants, vests, shirts, bodysuits, sweaters, tailored jackets, outerwear, and bras. Chapters 3 to 12 have diagrams that show you where and how to measure.

■ **Tables with Measurement Points.** These are for skirts, pants, vests, shirts, bodysuits, sweaters, tailored jackets, outerwear, and bras. Chapters 3 to 12 include charts that give written descriptions of where and how to measure.

1

Organization

Chapter 1 contains all the instructions you'll need to use *The Spec Manual.*

Chapter 2 features front and back view croquis figures for ten major categories. The use of exact measures for a sample size in each of the categories creates a unified and relative proportion for all figures.

Chapters 3 through 12 address how to measure and create spec sheets for a variety of garments. Each chapter deals with a particular silhouette and includes illustrated measurement points, a spec sheet template, and a table of measurement points. The flat sketches in these chapters were created using the croquis figures established in Chapter 2; the relative proportion between all figures and garment categories is consistent throughout the book.

Chapter 13, new to the second edition, addresses graphing garments utilizing data from sample spec sheets for various size and garment categories. This alternate and more advanced method of flat sketching illustrates appropriate values for the different measurement points. Garment graphs may be included with spec and grading sheets in more comprehensive spec packs.

Chapter 14, also new to the second edition, features a clip art library of flat sketches, pockets, collars, accessories, trim, and stitches.

The appendices contain a button selection gauge, graph templates (inches and centimeters), a metric conversion chart, a fraction to decimal conversion chart, and a grading worksheet that can be used in tandem with the incremental grade guides for all size categories.

Acknowledgments

We wish to thank the reviewers of the first edition proposal and manuscript for their many helpful suggestions. Thank you also to Irina Medvedenko whose advanced Illustrator skills were invaluable to the crafting of the new user-friendly clip art library. Olga Kontzias, Beth Cohen, and Barbara Chernow were enormously helpful in the revision, organization, and production of this second edition. We are grateful to Alexandra Armillas for her collaboration on the new specification sheet for a bra.

We also wish to acknowledge the help and support of our families during the planning and preparation of this book.

Michele Wesen Bryant and Diane DeMers

Preface

Please note: early print runs of this book included a CD-ROM; all content mentioned as part of the CD-ROM can now instead be accessed for free at https://www.bloomsburyfashioncentral.com/products/fairchild-books/studio-resources

The global supply chain and shrinking product lifecycles pose new challenges for apparel manufacturers. A single garment can be comprised of parts from all over the world (e.g., snaps from Germany, a zipper from Japan, and fabric from Taiwan). Assembly of the parts can also span the globe. Added to the mix are increasingly complex technical specifications for individual garments. The ability to flat sketch and write accurate specification sheets is more important than ever in order to create wearable clothing.

Our purpose in writing *The Spec Manual* is to provide fashion professionals and students with an affordable, up-to-date universal reference for croquis figures, points of measurement, and spec sheet templates. The second edition has been expanded to include instructions for measuring a fit model, a bra spec sheet, sample garment specs with plotted measurements, a grading worksheet, a clip art library, and grade guides for all size categories.

The Spec Manual, along with its accompanying CD-ROM, provides a uniform method for measuring garments and creating spec sheets. *The Spec Manual* is a tool that can be used in a variety of ways.

The text is organized as a workbook with all pages perforated for easy removal and archiving. These pages can then be used as templates, providing consistent formats for recordkeeping and/or homework.

In order to facilitate garment design and specification on the computer, *The Spec Manual* also includes a CD-ROM with croquis figures, spec sheet templates, a grading worksheet, and clip art. If you are not computer savvy, you can limit your use to hard copy. If you are working in a digital environment, you can use the CD-ROM to view and print files, enter data, and draw as your computer configuration allows. *The Spec Manual* is also a tool that enables the user to design original garments in all size categories.

In preparation for the second edition of *The Spec Manual,* we conducted an industry survey to determine current and future plans for the use of technology in fashion. Globalization and collaborative product management continue to be on the rise. We also determined that manual flat sketching and fashion specific proficiencies in Illustrator and Excel are frequently required of new employees. All of this supports our initial preference for off-the-shelf applications as a means for the broadest possible dissemination of design and production information. Students and designers working with limited access to proprietary systems are better served and can hone deeper skills by using less expensive and more ubiquitous off-the-shelf applications. Used in tandem with universal spreadsheet and drawing programs, the figures, templates, and clip art featured on *The Spec Manual* CD function as an affordable, user-friendly, portable alternative to proprietary PLM (product lifecycle management) systems.

Contents

FAIRCHILD BOOKS
Bloomsbury Publishing Inc
1385 Broadway, New York, NY 10018, USA
50 Bedford Square, London, WC1B 3DP, UK

BLOOMSBURY, FAIRCHILD BOOKS and the Fairchild Books logo
are trademarks of Bloomsbury Publishing Plc

First edition published 2001
This edition published 2006
Reprinted 2015, 2017, 2018, 2019 (twice), 2020

Cover design: Michele Wesen Bryant

Library of Congress Cataloging-in-Publication Data
LC record available at http://lccn.loc.gov/2005926489

ISBN: PB: 978-1-5636-7373-3
    ePDF: 978-1-5013-0894-9

Printed and bound in the United States of America

To find out more about our authors and books visit
www.fairchildbooks.com and sign up for our newsletter.

The Spec Manual
Second Edition

Michele Wesen Bryant
Fashion Institute of Technology

Diane DeMers
Fashion Institute of Technology

FAIRCHILD BOOKS
NEW YORK • LONDON • OXFORD • NEW DELHI • SYDNEY

The Spec Manual

The Spec Manual